For MacBook, MacBook Air and MacBook Pro

6th Edition
Updated for macOS High Sierra (v10.13)

In easy steps is an imprint of In Easy Steps Limited
16 Hamilton Terrace · Holly Walk · Leamington Spa
Warwickshire · United Kingdom · CV32 4LY
www.ineasysteps.com

Sixth Edition

Notice of Liability
Every effort has been made to ensure that this book contains accurate
and current information. However, In Easy Steps Limited and the
author shall not be liable for any loss or damage suffered by readers
as a result of any information contained herein.

Trademarks
OS X, macOS, MacBook, MacBook Air and MacBook Pro are registered
trademarks of Apple Computer, Inc. All other trademarks are
acknowledged as belonging to their respective companies.

In Easy Steps Limited supports The Forest Stewardship Council (FSC),
the leading international forest certification organization. All our titles
that are printed on Greenpeace approved FSC certified paper carry the
FSC logo.

MIX
Paper from
responsible sources
FSC® C020837

Printed and bound in the United Kingdom

ISBN 978-1-84078-794-8

Contents

1 Introducing MacBooks

Apple's MacBook range of laptop computers is stylish and user-friendly. This chapter introduces the MacBook range so you can choose the best one for your mobile computing needs.

About MacBooks

When Apple Computer, Inc. (renamed Apple Inc. in 1997) introduced its iMac range of desktop computers in 1998 it was a major breakthrough. To try to match the success of the iMac, Apple began working on a new range of notebook computers. It first entered this market seriously with the Macintosh Portable in 1989. In 1991, Apple introduced the PowerBook range of laptops, which was the forerunner to the MacBook range.

In 1999, a new range of Apple laptops was introduced. This was the iBook range, aimed firmly at the consumer market. In May 2006, the MacBook range first appeared. The two main reasons for this consolidation were:

- Simplifying Apple's laptop range under one banner.

- It was during this period that Apple Inc. was moving from Power PC processors for its computers, to Intel processors.

The MacBook range now consists of:

- **MacBook**. The latest standard MacBook model was launched in March 2015. It has a 12-inch Retina display screen and is designed to be as thin and as light as possible. It also has an innovative trackpad with Force Touch technology that provides extra functionality.

- **MacBook Pro**. This is the most powerful version of the MacBook, and two models contain the Touch Bar (introduced in 2016), for a range of added functionality from the keyboard.

- **MacBook Air**. This range was designed to be the thinnest and lightest on the market, and it is still an ultraportable laptop and ideal for mobile computing.

MacBooks had a lot of media coverage in terms of appearing in popular TV shows and movies. This has continued with the MacBook range.

The New icon indicates a new or enhanced feature introduced with the latest version of macOS High Sierra on the MacBook.

MacBook Models

Specifications for all computers change rapidly, and for the current MacBook range they are (at the time of printing):

MacBook
This has one model, with a 12-inch Retina display screen. There are two versions, with the following specifications:

- Processor: 1.2GHz or 1.3GHz dual-core Intel Core.

- Storage: 256GB or 512GB flash storage.

- Memory: 8GB of 1866MHz LPDDR3 onboard memory.

- Ports: USB-C, which can be used for charging and also as a USB 3.1 port for USB accessories.

MacBook Air
This has one model, with a 13-inch screen. There are two versions, with the following specifications:

- Processor: 1.8GHz or 2.2GHz dual-core Intel Core i5 or i7.

- Storage: 128GB or 256GB flash storage.

- Memory: 8GB of 1600MHz LPDDR3 onboard memory.

- Ports: Two USB 3.0 ports and one Thunderbolt 2 port.

MacBook Pro
This now contains the most extensive range, with standard 13- and 15-inch models and also 13- and 15-inch models with Touch Bar and Touch ID functionality (see pages 26-27 for details). The specifications for these models are:

- Processor: 13-inch, 2.3GHz or 3.1GHz dual-core Intel Core i5; 15-inch, 2.8GHZ or 2.9GHz dual-core Intel Core i7.

- Storage: 128GB, 256GB or 512GB flash storage.

- Memory: 13-inch, 8GB of 2133MHz LPDDR3 onboard memory; 15-inch, 16GB of 2133MHz LPDDR3 onboard memory.

- Ports: 13-inch, two or four Thunderbolt 3 (USB-C) ports and one USB 3.1 port; 15-inch, four Thunderbolt 3 ports and one USB 3.1 port.

All MacBooks have a range of energy-saving and environmental features.

The storage and memory on the MacBook range can both be configured to higher levels.

MacBook Air and the MacBook Pro both have flash storage. This is similar in some ways to traditional ROM (Read-Only Memory) storage, but it generally works faster and results in improved performance. The MacBook Pro Retina display is also designed with a flash architecture throughout to make it one of the most advanced laptops currently on the market.

9

MacBook Jargon Explained

Since MacBooks are essentially portable computers, a lot of the jargon is the same as for other computers. However, it is worth looking at some of this jargon and the significance it has in terms of MacBooks.

- **Processor**. Also known as the central processing unit, or CPU, this refers to the processing of digital data as it is provided by apps on the computer. The more powerful the processor, the quicker the data is interpreted. As with the rest of Apple's computers, MacBooks use Intel processors.

- **Memory**. This closely relates to the processor and is also known as random-access memory, or RAM. Essentially, this type of memory manages the apps that are being run and the commands that are being executed. The greater the amount of memory there is, the quicker the apps will run. With more RAM they will also be more stable and less likely to crash. In the current range of MacBooks, memory is measured in gigabytes (GB) and ranges from 4GB to 16GB.

- **Storage**. This refers to the amount of digital information the MacBook can store. It is frequently referred to in terms of hard disk space and is measured in gigabytes. MacBooks and MacBook Airs have flash memory.

- **Trackpad**. This is an input device that takes the place of a mouse (although a mouse can still be used with a MacBook, either with a USB cable or wirelessly). Traditionally, trackpads have come with a button that duplicates the function of the buttons on a mouse. However, the trackpad on a MacBook has no button, as the pad itself performs these functions.

Memory can be thought of as a temporary storage device, as it only keeps information about the currently-open apps. Storage is more permanent, as it keeps the information even when the MacBook has been turned off.

All MacBooks in the range, except the MacBook Air, have the Force Touch trackpad, which provides additional functionality for pressing on the trackpad.

● **Graphics card**. This is a device that enables images, video and animations to be displayed on the MacBook. It is also sometimes known as a video card. The faster the graphics card, the better the quality relevant media will be displayed at. In general, very fast graphics cards are really only needed for intensive multimedia applications, such as video games or videos. On a MacBook, this is an Intel graphics card.

● **Wireless**. This refers to a MacBook's ability to connect wirelessly to a network; i.e. another computer or an internet connection. In order to be able to do this the MacBook must have a wireless card, which enables it to connect to a network or high-speed internet connection. This is known as the AirPort Extreme Wi-Fi wireless networking card.

● **Bluetooth**. This is a radio technology for connecting devices wirelessly over short distances. It can be used for items such as a wireless mouse, or for connecting to a device, such as an iPhone for downloading photos.

● **Ports**. These are the parts of a MacBook that external devices can be plugged into, using a cable such as a USB or a Thunderbolt port. They are located on the side of the MacBook.

The new MacBook has one USB-C port, which can be used for charging and external USB devices.

● **USB**. This is a method for connecting a variety of external devices, such as digital cameras; MP3 music players; scanners; and printers. The latest range of MacBooks uses USB 3.1.

● **Ethernet**. This is for connecting an Ethernet cable to a router, for accessing the internet, rather than doing it wirelessly.

Don't forget

USB stands for Universal Serial Bus and is a popular way of connecting external devices to computers.

...cont'd

- **Thunderbolt**. This is a port for transferring data at high speeds, even faster than FireWire (which has been used previously on MacBooks). It can also be used to attach a Thunderbolt Display monitor.

- **Touch Bar**. This is available on the latest models of the 13-inch and 15-inch MacBook Pro. It is a multi-touch strip located at the top of the keyboard that offers a range of options, depending on the current app being used; e.g. the system controls, such as for adjusting volume and screen brightness, or adding emojis to an iMessage.

Don't forget

For more details about the Touch Bar, see pages 26-27.

The Touch Bar also contains the On/Off button (at the far right-hand side) and can display the function keys (by holding down the Fn key on the keyboard).

- **CD/DVD players or re-writers**. The latest range of MacBooks, MacBook Airs and MacBook Pros with Retina display do not have a built-in CD/DVD player or re-writer. However, an external USB SuperDrive can be purchased for playing DVDs and CDs or burning content to a CD or DVD. For copying content, flashdrives are also a popular option as they can contain large amounts of data and connect via a USB port.

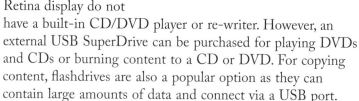

Don't forget

When a USB SuperDrive is attached to a MacBook, it shows up as an external drive in the Finder; see page 32.

- **Webcam (FaceTime)**. This is a type of camera fitted into the MacBook and it can be used to take still photographs or communicate via video with other people. On the MacBook it is known as the FaceTime camera, and it works with the FaceTime app. The FaceTime camera is built-in at the top-middle of the inner casing.

Getting Comfortable

Since you will probably be using your MacBook in more than one location, the issue of finding a comfortable working position can be vital, particularly as you cannot put the keyboard and monitor in different positions, as you can with a desktop computer. Whenever you are using your MacBook, try to make sure that you are sitting in a comfortable position, with your back well supported, and that the MacBook is in a position where you can reach the keyboard easily, and also see the screen, without straining your arms.

Despite the possible temptation to do so, avoid using your MacBook in bed, on your lap, or where you have to slouch or strain to reach the MacBook properly.

Seating position

The ideal way to sit at a MacBook is with an office-type chair that offers good support for your back. Even with these types of chairs, it is important to maintain a good body position so that your back is straight and your head is pointing forwards.

If possible, the best place to work on a MacBook is at a dedicated desk or workstation.

One of the advantages of office-type chairs is that the height can usually be adjusted, and this can be a great help in achieving a comfortable position.

If you do not have an office-type chair, use a chair with a straight back and place a cushion behind you for extra support and comfort, as required.

...cont'd

MacBook position

When working at your MacBook it is important to have it positioned so that both the keyboard and the screen are in a comfortable position. If the keyboard is too low, you will have to slouch or strain to reach it.

If the keyboard is too high, your arms will be stretching. This could lead to pain in your tendons.

The ideal setup is to have the MacBook in a position where you can sit with your forearms and wrists as level as possible while you are typing on the keyboard.

Adjusting the screen

Another factor in working comfortably at a MacBook is the position of the screen. Unlike a desktop computer, it is not feasible to have a MacBook screen at eye level, as this would result in the keyboard being in too high a position. Instead, once you have achieved a comfortable seating position, open the screen so that it is approximately 90 degrees from your eyeline.

Don't forget

Working comfortably at a MacBook involves a combination of a good chair, good posture and good MacBook positioning.

One potential issue with MacBook screens can be that they reflect glare from sunlight or indoor lighting.

If this happens, either change your position, or block out the light source using some form of blind or shade. Avoid squinting at a screen that is reflecting glare, as this will make you feel uncomfortable and quickly give you a headache.

Input Devices

MacBooks have the same data input devices as most laptops: a keyboard and a trackpad. However, the trackpad has an innovative feature that makes it stand out from the crowd: there is no button – the trackpad itself performs the functions of a button. The trackpad uses Multi-Touch Gestures to replace traditional navigation techniques. These are looked at in detail in Chapter 6. Some of these gestures are:

- **One-finger click**. Click in the middle of the trackpad to perform one-click operations.

- **Scrolling**. This can be done on a page by dragging two fingers on the trackpad either up or down.

- **Zooming on a page or web page**. This can be done by double-tapping with two fingers.

When using the keyboard or trackpad, keep your hands and fingers as flat as possible over the keyboard and trackpad.

Trackpad options

Options for the functioning of the trackpad can be set within **System Preferences** (see pages 28-29). To do this:

1 Click on the **Trackpad** button

2 Click on the tabs to set options for pointing and clicking, scrolling and zooming, and additional Multi-Touch Gestures with the trackpad

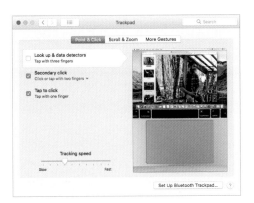

...cont'd

Mouse options

An external mouse can be connected to a MacBook, and options for its functioning can be set within **System Preferences**. To do this:

Hot tip

Instead of a traditional mouse, a Magic Mouse can also be connected to a MacBook. This is a wireless mouse that connects via Bluetooth and has the same scrolling functionality as the trackpad.

1 Click on the **Mouse** button

2 Drag the sliders to set the speed at which the cursor moves across the screen, and also the speed required for a double-click operation

Keyboard options

Options for the functioning of the keyboard can be set within **System Preferences.** To do this:

1 Click on the **Keyboard** button

2 Click on the **Keyboard** tab to set options for how the keyboard operates, such as the speed for repeating a key stroke

3 Click on the **Text** tab to set keyboard shortcuts for accessing certain words and phrases. Click on this button to add a new shortcut and phrase

MacBook Power Cable

All MacBooks need a power cable, in the form of an AC adapter that can be used to recharge the battery, and it can also be used when the MacBook is not being used in a mobile environment. This can save the battery so, if possible, the adapter should be used instead of battery power.

The MacBook adapter also has a built-in safety feature known as the MagSafe power port. This consists of a magnetic connection between the power adapter and the power port on the side of the MacBook. When the connection is made, it is a magnetic one rather than a physical one. This means that if the power cord is accidentally pulled or kicked out, the magnetic connection will be broken without dragging the MacBook with it. This is safer for both the user and the MacBook itself.

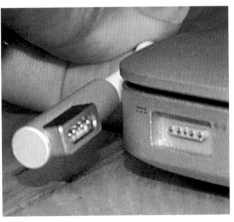

Hot tip

The MacBook power cable has a light on the end of the magnetic connector. When the cable is plugged in, this appears amber if the MacBook is charging, and green when the charging is complete.

Cleaning a MacBook

Like most things, MacBooks benefit greatly from a little care and attention. The two most important areas to keep clean are the screen and the keyboard.

Cleaning the screen

All computer screens quickly collect dust and fingerprints, and MacBooks are no different. If this is left too long, it can make the screen harder to read and cause eye strain and headaches. Clean the screen regularly with the following cleaning materials:

- A lint-free cloth, similar to the type used to clean camera lenses (it is important not to scratch the screen in any way).

- An alcohol-free cleaning fluid recommended for computer screens.

- Screen wipes that are recommended for use on computer screens.

Cleaning the keyboard

Keyboards are notorious for accumulating dust, fluff and crumbs. One way to solve this problem is to turn the MacBook upside down and very gently shake it to loosen any foreign objects. Failing this, a can of compressed air can be used, with a narrow nozzle to blow out any stubborn items that remain lodged between the keys.

Don't forget

The outer casing of a MacBook can be cleaned with the same fluid as used for the screen. A duster or a damp (but not wet) cloth and warm water can be equally effective. Keep soap away from MacBooks if possible.

18

Spares and Accessories

Whenever you are going anywhere with your MacBook, there are always spares and accessories to consider. Some of these are just nice things to have, while others could be essential in ensuring that you can still use your MacBook if anything goes wrong while you are on your travels. Items to consider putting in your MacBook case include:

Hardware

- **Spare battery**. This is probably the most important spare if you are going to be away from home or work for any length of time, and particularly if you think you may be unable to access a power supply for a long period of time and be unable to charge your MacBook battery. Like all batteries, MacBook batteries slowly lose power over time and do not keep their charge for as long as when they are new. It is a good idea to always keep an eye on how much battery power you have left and, if you are running low, to try to conserve as much energy as possible (see Chapter 11).

- **Apple Thunderbolt Display**. The Thunderbolt port enables you to transfer data from peripheral devices to your MacBook at very high speeds. You can also connect a Thunderbolt Display – a 27-inch display that can give stunning clarity to the content on your monitor.

- **Magic Mouse**. This is an external mouse that can be connected to your MacBook and used to perform Multi-Touch Gestures in the same way as the trackpad.

- **External SuperDrive**. The MacBook range does not come with a SuperDrive for using CDs and DVDs but this external one can be used to connect to a MacBook using a USB cable.

- **Wireless keyboard**. This can be used if you want to have a keyboard that you can move away from your MacBook.

- **USB Ethernet adapter**. This can be used to connect to an Ethernet network using a USB port.

- **Multi-card reader**. This is a device that can be used to copy data from the cards used in digital cameras. If you have a digital camera, it is possible to download the photographs from it directly onto a MacBook with a cable. However, a multi-card reader can be more efficient and flexible.

Beware

MacBook batteries should only be fitted by authorized Apple suppliers for an Apple Store. If you try to fit one yourself, it may invalidate the MacBook's warranty.

...cont'd

It is important that headphones are comfortable to wear for extended periods of time. In general, the types that fit over the ears are more comfortable than the "bud" variety that are inserted into the ear.

The App Store can be accessed by clicking on this button on the Dock at the bottom of the MacBook screen.

- **Headphones**. These can be used to listen to music or films if you are in the company of other people and you do not want to disturb them. They can also be very useful if there are distracting noises from other people.

- **Flashdrive**. This is a small device that can be used to copy data to and from your MacBook. It connects via a USB port and is about the size of a packet of chewing gum. It is an excellent way of backing up files from your MacBook when you are away from home or the office.

- **Cleaning material**. The materials described on page 18 can be taken to ensure your MacBook is always in tip-top condition for use.

- **DVDs/CDs**. Video or music DVDs and CDs can be taken to provide mobile entertainment, and blank ones can be taken to copy data onto, similar to using a pen drive. An external DVD/CD drive will also be required.

Software

New software programs, or apps, can be downloaded directly from the Mac App Store. There is a huge range on offer, covering over 20 different categories. They can be searched for by **Featured**, **Top Charts** and **Categories** and you can also view and update apps that you have purchased (see pages 131-136).

2 Around a MacBook

This chapter looks at getting started with your MacBook: from opening it up and turning it on, through to keyboard functions and the System Preferences.

It also looks at the Touch Bar (available on some models).

Opening Up

The first step towards getting started with a new MacBook is to open it ready for use.

There is no physical latch on the front of a MacBook; just a small groove at the front where the top and bottom parts meet.

Instead of a latch, a MacBook has a magnetic closing mechanism, which engages when the monitor screen is closed onto the main body of the MacBook. To open it, raise it firmly upwards from the center, where there is a smooth groove.

Once the MacBook has been opened, the screen should stay in whatever position it is placed.

Beware

Open the screen of a MacBook carefully, so as not to put any unnecessary pressure on the connection between the screen and the main body of the MacBook.

Don't forget

To turn on the MacBook, press the button in the top right-hand corner of the keyboard.

On models with the Touch Bar, this button is located at the right-hand side of the bar.

22

MacBook Desktop

The opening view of a MacBook is known as the Desktop. Items such as apps and files can be stored on the Desktop but, in general, it is best to try to keep it as clear as possible.

At the top of the Desktop is the Apple menu (Apple symbol) and the Menu bar. This contains links to a collection of commonly-used menus and functions, such as Copy and Paste.

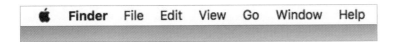

At the bottom of the Desktop is the Dock. This is a collection of icons that are shortcuts to frequently-used apps or folders.

One of the items on the Dock is the Finder. This can be used to access the main area for apps, folders and files, and also to organize the way you work on your MacBook.

The menus on the Menu bar are looked at in detail on page 100.

To specify which items appear on the Desktop, click on **Finder > Preferences** on the Menu bar. Click on the **General** tab and select to show or hide **Hard disks**, **External disks**, **CDs, DVDs and iPods** or **Connected servers**. The selected items will then be displayed as icons on the Desktop.

Apple Menu

The Apple menu is accessed from the Apple symbol at the left-hand side of the Menu bar:

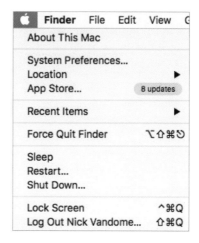

The options on the Apple menu are:

- **About This Mac**. This provides general information about the processor, the amount of memory and the High Sierra version.

- **System Preferences**. This is a shortcut to System Preferences. This can be used to access a wide range of options, including those for items such as the Dock.

- **App Store**. This can be used to access the online Mac App Store for downloading apps, and also software updates for existing apps and High Sierra.

- **Recent Items**. This displays the items you have most recently used and viewed.

- **Force Quit**. This can be used to manually quit an app that has frozen or will not close.

- **Sleep**. This puts the MacBook into a state of hibernation.

- **Restart**. This closes down the MacBook and restarts it.

- **Shut Down**. This shuts down the MacBook.

- **Log Out**. This shuts down the currently-open apps, and logs out the current user.

Hot tip

Force Quit can be used to close down an app that is frozen or is not responding.

Standard Keyboard Buttons

A MacBook keyboard has a number of keys that can be used for shortcuts or specific functions. Four of them are located at the left of the space bar. They are (from left to right):

- **The Function key**. This can be used to activate the function (Fn) keys at the top of the keyboard: press the Fn key and the required F key at the same time.

- **The Control key**. This can be used to access contextual menus.

- **The Alt (Option) key**. This is frequently used in conjunction with the Command key to perform specific tasks.

- **The Command key**. As above.

At the top of the keyboard there are F keys for changing some of the settings on your MacBook. These are (from left to right):

- F1: Decrease brightness.

- F2: Increase brightness.

- F3: Show all open windows (Mission Control).

- F4: Show/Hide Dashboard widgets.

- F7: Rewind a video.

- F8: Play/Pause a video.

- F9: Fast-forward a video (with Fn key, shows all open windows: Mission Control).

- F10: Mute volume (with Fn key, displays all open windows for the active app).

- F11: Decrease volume (with Fn key, displays the Desktop and minimizes all windows around the sides of the screen).

- F12: Increase volume (with Fn key, displays the Dashboard).

Contextual menus are ones that have actions that are specific to the item being viewed.

The **F5** and **F6** keys on the MacBook can be used, respectively, to decrease and increase the brightness of the backlighting on the keyboard.

On models of MacBook with the Touch Bar, the F keys appear on the Touch Bar rather than physically on the keyboard.

Touch Bar

The Touch Bar is an innovation that is included with the compatible versions of the 13-inch and 15-inch models of the MacBook Pro. It is a glass strip at the top of the keyboard that offers multi-touch dynamic functionality, tailored to the app being used. It operates in a similar way to the screen of a smartphone, such as the iPhone, in that options can be accessed by tapping and swiping on it. The Touch Bar also includes Touch ID functionality (at the far right-hand side of the Touch Bar), which can be used to unlock the MacBook using a fingerprint (in the same way as it is used on an iPhone and an iPad).

Hot tip

The area on the far right-hand side of the Touch Bar can be used to turn on the MacBook, unlock it with Touch ID, and also pay for online items with Apple Pay at participating retailers.

Using the Touch Bar

The Touch Bar options change according to which app is currently being used. Also, some apps have additional options that can be accessed by swiping from right to left on the Touch Bar.

Don't forget

More apps are being created by third-party developers that support Touch Bar functionality so, in time, there will be more and more apps that can be used with the Touch Bar.

Although the options on the Touch Bar change with different apps, there are some default buttons that appear on some of the Touch Bar options, but not all of them. These are for amending brightness and volume, and accessing Siri. Tap on the left-pointing arrow to expand these options.

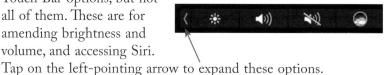

Touch Bar options

Some of the Touch Bar options, for specific apps, include:

General Settings: This can be used to change screen brightness and contrast, access Mission Control for viewing open apps, use video controls and adjust volume.

Web pages – Safari app: This can be used to move between the previous and next web pages, search the web, access different tabs in Safari, view tabs and add new tabs.

Email – Mail app: This can be used to create, format and send email messages.

Text messages – Messages app: This can be used to add a range of emojis to text messages.

Color selection – Keynote, Pages, Photoshop and other apps with color selection: This can be used to make color selection with a slider or color wheel for apps that have this option.

F keys: The traditional F keys are available on the Touch Bar by pressing the Fn key on the keyboard.

System Preferences

In macOS High Sierra there are preferences that can be set for just about every aspect of the operating system. This gives you great control over how the interface looks and how the operating system functions. To access System Preferences:

 Click on this icon on the Dock or from the Applications folder in the Finder

Don't forget

For more information about the Dock, see pages 54-63; and for the Finder, see Chapter 5.

Personal preferences

General. Options for the overall look of buttons, menus, windows and scroll bars.

Desktop & Screen Saver. This can be used to change the Desktop background and the screen saver.

Dock. Options for the way the Dock looks and functions.

Mission Control. This gives you a variety of options for managing all of your open windows and apps.

Language & Region. Options for the language used.

Security & Privacy. This enables you to secure your Home folder with a master password, for added security.

Spotlight. This can be used to specify settings for the High Sierra search facility, Spotlight.

Notifications. This can be used to set up how you are notified about items such as email, messages and software updates.

Hot tip

When viewing a specific System Preference, click on this button at the top of the window to go back to all of the available options.

Hardware preferences

CDs & DVDs. Options for what action is taken when you insert CDs and DVDs.

Displays. Options for the screen display, such as resolution.

Energy Saver. Options for when the computer is inactive.

Keyboard. Options for how the keyboard functions, and also keyboard shortcuts.

Mouse. Options for how an external mouse functions.

Trackpad. Options for when you are using the trackpad.

Printers & Scanners. Options for selecting and installing printers and scanners.

Sound. Options for adding sound effects and for playing and recording sound.

Startup Disk. This can be used to specify the disk from which your computer starts up. This is usually the High Sierra volume.

Internet & Wireless preferences
iCloud. Options for the online iCloud service.

Internet Accounts. This can be used to set up online services on your MacBook, including social media accounts.

App Store. This can be used to connect to the App Store to access and install available software updates.

Network. This can be used to specify network settings for linking two or more computers together.

Bluetooth. Options for attaching Bluetooth wireless devices.

Extensions. This determines how plug-ins and extensions are installed on your MacBook.

Sharing. Options for selecting how files are shared on a network.

System preferences
Users & Groups. This can be used to allow different users to create their own accounts for use on the same computer.

Parental Controls. This can be used to limit access to the MacBook and to various online functions and services.

Siri. This has options for how the built-in digital voice assistant, Siri, can be used.

Date & Time. Options for changing the computer's date and time to time zones around the world.

Time Machine. This can be used to configure and set up the High Sierra backup facility.

Accessibility. This can be used to set options for users who have difficulty with viewing text on screen, hearing commands, using the keyboard or using the mouse.

Hot tip

The headings for System Preferences shown here are how they are grouped by default, although the headings themselves do not appear. To change the way System Preferences is organized, click on **View** on the System Preferences Menu bar and select either **Organize by Categories** or **Organize Alphabetically**.

CDs and DVDs

Although there is no built-in SuperDrive with the latest range of MacBook Air and MacBook Pro versions, CDs and DVDs can still be used with an external USB SuperDrive. As with many of the functions of a MacBook, there are settings that can be applied within System Preferences. To do this:

1 Open **System Preferences** and click on the **CDs & DVDs** button

CDs & DVDs

2 There are various options for what happens when you insert blank CDs/DVDs, and also for music, picture and video CDs/DVDs

USB flashdrives can also be used if you want to copy content from a MacBook.

3 If you insert a blank CD or DVD, the following window appears automatically. The **Action:** box offers options for what you want to do with the CD or DVD. Click on the **OK** button to select an action, or click on the **Ignore** button if you do not want to use any of these actions

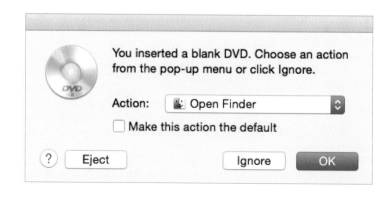

Connecting a Printer

Using a printer on any computer is essential, and MacBooks allow you to quickly add a printer to aid your productivity. To do this:

1 Open **System Preferences** and click on the **Printers & Scanners** button

2 Currently-installed printers are displayed in the **Printers** list

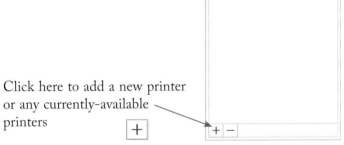

3 Click here to add a new printer or any currently-available printers

4 Select a printer and click on the **Add** button

5 macOS High Sierra loads the required printer driver. (If it does not have a specific one it will try to use a generic one)

6 The details about the printer are available in the **Printers** window

Printer drivers are programs that enable the printer to communicate with your computer. Printer drivers are usually provided on a disc when the printer is purchased. In addition, MacBooks will have a number of printer drivers pre-installed. If your MacBook does not recognize your printer, you can load the driver from the disc.

Once a printer has been installed, documents can be printed by selecting **File** > **Print** from the Menu bar. Print settings can be set at this point, and they can also be set by selecting **File** > **Page/Print Setup** from the Menu bar in most apps.

External Drives

Attaching external drives is an essential part of mobile computing, whether it is to back up data as you are traveling, or for downloading photos and other items. On MacBooks, external drives are displayed on the Desktop once they have been attached, and they can then be used for the required task. To do this:

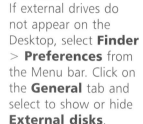
 Attach the external drive. This is usually done with a USB cable. Once it has been attached, it is shown on the Desktop

The drive is shown in the Finder

Perform the required task for the external drive (such as copying files or folders onto it from the hard drive of your MacBook)

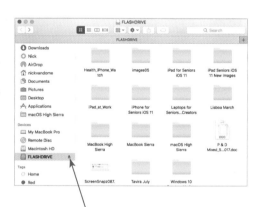

External drives should be ejected properly, not just pulled out or removed. To do this, click on this button next to the drive in the Finder window, or drag its icon on the Desktop over the **Trash** icon on the Dock. This will then change into an **Eject** icon, and the drive can then be removed

32

3 Introducing High Sierra

High Sierra is the latest operating system for MacBooks. This chapter introduces some of its essential features so that you can quickly feel comfortable using it. It also covers the digital voice assistant, Siri, which is included on MacBooks.

macOS High Sierra is the latest version of the Mac operating system.

UNIX is an operating system that has traditionally been used for large commercial mainframe computers. It is renowned for its stability and ability to be used within different computing environments.

High Sierra has a Power Nap function that updates items from the online iCloud service even when a MacBook is in Sleep mode. This can be set up by checking **On** the **Wake for Network Access** option in the **Energy Saver** section of System Preferences.

About macOS High Sierra

macOS High Sierra is the 13th version (10.13) of the operating system for Apple computers: the iMac, MacBook, Mac Mini and Mac Pro. Although it is still a development of the OS X (pronounced "ten") operating system for Macs, the naming convention has been changed to macOS, to more clearly identify it as belonging to the Mac, rather than a mobile device such as the iPad or iPhone. Like earlier versions, it is based on the UNIX programming language, which is a very stable and secure operating environment and ensures that macOS is one of the most stable consumer operating systems that has ever been designed. More importantly for the user, it is also one of the most stylish and user-friendly operating systems available.

When one of macOS High Sierra's predecessors, OS X Mountain Lion, was introduced in 2012, it contained a range of innovative functions that were inspired by Apple's mobile devices: iPhone, iPad and iPod Touch. This was continued with the next versions of the operating system: OS X Yosemite, OS X El Capitan, macOS Sierra and now macOS High Sierra. The three main areas where the functionality of the mobile devices has been transferred to the desktop and laptop operating system are:

- The way apps can be downloaded and installed. Instead of using a disc, macOS High Sierra utilizes the App Store to provide apps, which can be installed in a couple of steps.

- Options for navigating around pages and applications on a trackpad or a Magic Mouse. Instead of having to use a mouse or a traditional laptop trackpad, macOS High Sierra uses Multi-Touch Gestures for navigating apps and web pages.

- Siri, Apple's digital voice assistant, has now made the transition from being only available on mobile devices to being included with macOS High Sierra too.

macOS High Sierra continues the evolution of the operating system, by adding more features and enhancing the ones that were already there. These include: enhancements to the Photos app, making it easier to find photos according to people and places, and enhanced editing functions for manipulating photos; a wider range of emojis for adding to Messages; and enhancements to the Notes app for pinning notes and adding tables.

Installing macOS High Sierra

When it comes to installing macOS High Sierra you do not need to worry about an installation CD or DVD; it can be downloaded and installed directly from the online App Store. New MacBooks will have macOS High Sierra installed, and the following range is compatible with macOS High Sierra and can be upgraded with it:

- MacBook (Late 2009 or newer).

- MacBook Pro (2010 or newer).

- MacBook Air (2010 or newer).

If you want to install macOS High Sierra on an existing MacBook, you will need to have the minimum requirements of:

- OS X Lion (10.7.5) or later (see first tip).

- Intel Core 2 Duo; Core i3; Core i5; Core i7; or Xeon processor, or higher.

- 2GB of memory and 8.8GB of available storage for installation.

If your MacBook meets these requirements, you can download and install macOS High Sierra, for free, as follows:

1 Click on this icon on the Dock to access the App Store (or select **Software Update**... – see Hot tip)

2 Locate the **macOS High Sierra** icon (this will be on the **Featured** page or within the **Utilities** category)

3 Click on the **Download** button and follow the installation instructions

Download ▼

macOS High Sierra is a free upgrade from the App Store if you already have the Lion, Mountain Lion, Mavericks, Yosemite or El Capitan versions of OS X, or macOS Sierra on your Mac.

macOS High Sierra is a new version of the Mac operating system. It contains a number of new technologies to make the operating system faster and more reliable than ever.

To check your computer's software version and upgrade options, click on **Apple menu** > **About This Mac** from the main Menu bar. Click on the **Overview** tab and click on the **Software Update...** button. See page 39 for details.

The High Sierra Environment

The first most noticeable element about High Sierra is its elegant user interface. This has been designed to create a user-friendly graphic overlay to the UNIX operating system at the heart of High Sierra, and it is a combination of rich colors and sharp, original graphics. The main elements that make up the initial High Sierra environment are:

Apple menu   Menu bar menus   Windows   Menu bar icons

The Dock   Desktop

The Dock is designed to help make organizing and opening items as quick and easy as possible. For a detailed look at the Dock, see pages 54-63.

Many of the behind-the-scenes features of macOS High Sierra are aimed at saving power on your MacBook. These include timer-coalescing technologies for saving processing and battery power; features for saving energy when apps are not being used; power-saving features in Safari for ignoring additional content provided by web page plug-ins; and memory compression to make your MacBook quicker and more responsive.

The **Apple menu** is standardized throughout High Sierra, regardless of the app in use.

Menus

Menus in High Sierra contain commands for the operating system and any relevant apps. If there is an arrow next to a command it means there are subsequent options for the item. Some menus also incorporate the same transparency as the sidebar so that the background shows through.

Transparency

One feature in macOS High Sierra is that the sidebar and toolbars in certain apps are transparent so that you can see some of the screen behind it. This also helps the uppermost window blend in with the background:

1 In certain apps with a sidebar, such as the Finder or the Safari sidebar, the background appears behind the sidebar

2 When you move the window, the background behind the sidebar changes accordingly

Don't forget

The red window button is used to close a window. However, this does not quit the app. The amber button is used to minimize a window, so that it appears at the right-hand side of the Dock.

Window buttons

These appear in any open macOS window, and can be used to manipulate the window. They sometimes include a full-screen option. Use the window button to, from left to right, close a window, minimize a window, or maximize a window.

If an app has full-screen functionality, this green button is available:

About Your MacBook

When you buy a new MacBook you will almost certainly check the technical specifications before you make a purchase. Once you have your MacBook, there will be times when you will want to view these specifications again, such as the version of macOS in use, the amount of memory, and the amount of storage. This can be done through the **About This Mac** option that can be accessed from the Apple menu. To do this:

1 Click on the **Apple menu** and click on the **About This Mac** link

2 Click on the **Overview** tab

3 This window contains information about the version of macOS being used; processor; amount of memory; type of graphics card; and serial number

4 Click on the **System Report...** button to view full details about the hardware and software on your MacBook

Hot tip

The System Report section is also where you can check whether your MacBook is compatible with the Handoff functionality (covered on page 69), although this does not work with most Macs before 2012. Click on the **Bluetooth** section in the **System Report** to see if Handoff is supported.

...cont'd

5 Click on the **Software Update...** button to see available software updates for your MacBook

Display information
This gives information about your MacBook's display:

1 Click on the **Displays** tab

For more information about setting Software Updates, see page 181.

2 This window contains information about your display including the type, size, resolution and graphics card

3 Click on the **Displays Preferences...** button to view options for changing the display's resolution, brightness and color

...cont'd

Storage information

This contains information about your MacBook's physical and removable storage:

1 Click on the **Storage** tab   Storage

Click on the **Manage...** button in the Storage window to view how much space specific apps are taking up, and also options for optimizing storage on your Mac. With macOS High Sierra, this is known as **Optimized Storage**, which is accessed from the **Details** tab from within **Storage** > **Manage**. Optimized Storage includes a **Store in iCloud** option, which can be used to enable your Mac to identify files that have not been opened or used in a long time and then automatically store them in iCloud (if you have enough storage space there). Their location remains the same on your Mac, but they are physically kept in iCloud, thus freeing up more space on your Mac. Optimized Storage also has options for removing iTunes movies and TV shows that have been watched, emptying the Trash automatically, and reducing overall clutter on your Mac.

2 This window contains information about the used and available storage on your hard disk, and also options for writing various types of CDs and DVDs

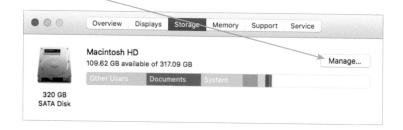

Memory information

This contains information about your MacBook's memory, which is used to run macOS and also the applications on your computer:

1 Click on the **Memory** tab   Memory

2 This window contains information about the memory chips that are in your MacBook

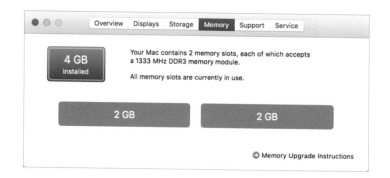

40

3 Click on the **Memory Upgrade Instructions** if you want to upgrade your memory

4 A page on the Apple website gives instructions for upgrading memory chips for different makes and models of Macs

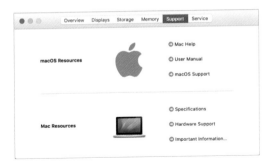

Always wear an anti-static wristband if you are opening your MacBook to insert new memory chips, or any other time when you are working on the components of your MacBook, otherwise you could cause electrical damage to your MacBook.

Support

The **Support** tab provides links to a range of help options for your MacBook and macOS.

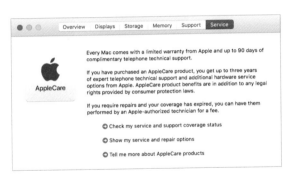

Service

The **Service** tab provides links to service and repair options and also the AppleCare Protection Plan, for extending the initial one-year warranty for your MacBook.

Customizing Your MacBook

Background imagery is an important way to add your own personal touch to your MacBook. (This is the graphical element upon which all other items on your computer sit.) There is a range of background options that can be used. To select your own background and screen saver:

1 Click on the **Desktop & Screen Saver** button in **System Preferences**

Desktop & Screen Saver

2 Click on the **Desktop** tab

Desktop

3 Select a location from where you want to select a background

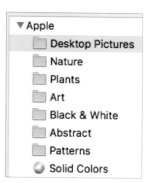

▼ Apple
📁 Desktop Pictures
📁 Nature
📁 Plants
📁 Art
📁 Black & White
📁 Abstract
📁 Patterns
⬤ Solid Colors

Don't forget

You can select your own photographs as your Desktop background, once you have loaded them onto your MacBook. To do this, select the Photos folder in Step 3 and browse to the photograph you want.

4 Click on one of the available backgrounds

5 The background is applied as the Desktop background imagery

6 Click on the **Screen Saver** tab

7 Click in the **Source:** box to select a source for the screen saver design. Click in the left-hand panel to select how the screen saver operates

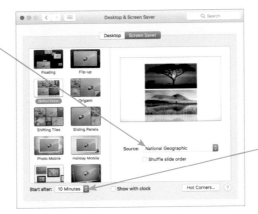

Click in the screen saver **Start after:** box to specify a period of time of inactivity after which the screen saver starts.

General customization

Other customization options can be found in the General section of System Preferences:

1 Click on the **General** button in the **System Preferences** folder

2 The General window has options for items including changing the appearance of buttons, menus and windows; changing highlight colors; specifying when scroll bars appear; and setting the default web browser

43

Using Siri

Available with macOS High Sierra, Siri is the digital voice assistant that can be used to vocally search for a wide range of items from your MacBook and the web. Also, the results can be managed in innovative ways so that keeping up-to-date is easier than ever.

Setting up Siri

To set up and start using Siri:

In macOS High Sierra, Siri has been updated with a more natural voice and a greater range of intonations and expressions.

44

Check **On** the **Show Siri in menu bar** box to show the Siri icon in the top right-hand corner of the main Apple Menu bar.

☑ Show Siri in menu bar

An internal or external microphone is required in order to ask Siri questions.

1 Open **System Preferences** and click on the **Siri** button

2 Check **On** the **Enable Ask Siri** box

3 Make selections here for how Siri operates, including language and the voice used by Siri

4 Click on the **Siri** icon on the Dock or in the Menu bar to open Siri

5 The Siri window opens, ready for use

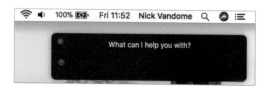

Searching with Siri

Siri can respond to most requests, including playing a music track, checking the weather, opening photos, and adding calendar events. If you open Siri but do not ask a question, it will prompt you with a list of possible queries. Click on the microphone icon at the bottom of the panel to ask a question. It is also possible to ask questions of Siri while you are working on another document.

Siri can search for a vast range of items, from your MacBook or the web. Some useful Siri functions include:

Searching for documents
This can be refined by specifying documents covering a particular date or subject:

1 Ask Siri to find and display documents with a criteria; e.g. created by a specific person

2 Ask Siri to refine the criteria; e.g. only include documents from a specific date range. Click on an item to open it in its related app

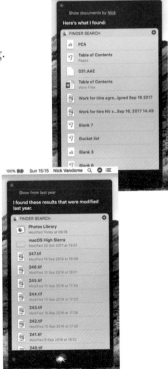

Searching for documents using Siri is a new feature in macOS High Sierra.

It is possible to ask Siri to search for specific types of documents; e.g. those created in Pages, or PDF files.

...cont'd

Drag and drop results

Once search results have been displayed by Siri, they can be managed in a variety of ways. One of these is to copy an item in the search results into another app, by dragging and dropping:

Click on the cross in the top left-hand corner of the Siri window to close it. Otherwise, it can be left open for more queries and searches.

1 Ask Siri to display a certain type of item, such as a map location or an image

2 Drag the resulting item into another app, such as a word processing app or the Notes app

Multitasking

The Siri search window can be left open on the Desktop so that you can ask Siri a question while you are working on something else; e.g. while you are working on a document, ask Siri to display a relevant web page.

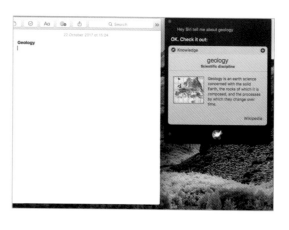

Pinning results

Some search results are dynamic; i.e. they change on a regular basis. This includes items such as sports results and weather forecasts. With Siri, these can be pinned to the Notification Center and they will then be updated when they change. To pin Siri search results:

1 Search for a certain item, such as the results of your favorite sports team

2 When Siri returns the result, click on this button to pin the search to the Notification Center

3 The item will be pinned to the Notifications Center, which will always display the most recent information and will be updated when new details are available

Hot tip

For more information about using the Notification Center, see page 130.

47

Search Options

In addition to Siri, there are two other options for searching for items on a MacBook with macOS High Sierra:

Spotlight search

Spotlight is the dedicated search app for macOS. It can be used over all the files on your MacBook and the internet. To use Spotlight:

Spotlight starts searching for items as soon as you start typing a word. So don't worry if some of the first results look inappropriate, as these will disappear once you have finished typing the full word.

1 Click on this icon towards the far right of the Apple menu bar

2 Click in the Spotlight search box

3 Enter a keyword or phrase for which you want to search

4 The top hits from within your apps are shown in the left-hand panel. Click on one to view its details

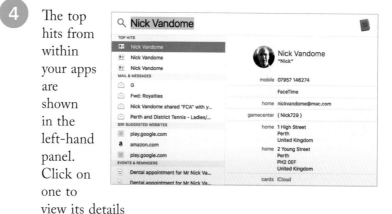

Don't forget

Spotlight search can show results from your MacBook; the internet; iTunes; the App Store; and also items such as movies nearby and local restaurants. These are displayed on a map within the Spotlight search results.

5 Scroll down the left-hand panel to view different search result options, such as entries from Wikipedia or the web, or a dictionary definition of a word

Finder search

This is the search box in the top right-hand corner of the Finder, and can be used to search for items within it. See page 92 for details about using Finder search.

Accessibility

In all areas of computing it is important to give as many people access to the system as possible. This includes users with visual impairments and also people who have problems using the mouse and keyboard. In macOS this is achieved through the functions of the **Accessibility** System Preferences. To use these:

1 Click on the **Accessibility** button in **System Preferences**

2 Click on the **Display** button for options for changing the display colors and contrast, and for increasing the cursor size

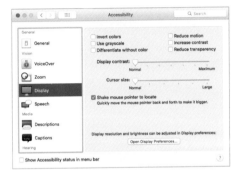

3 Click on the **Zoom** button for options to zoom in on the screen

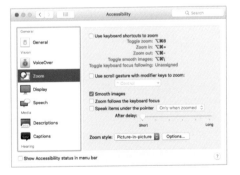

Experiment with the VoiceOver function, if only to see how it operates. This will give you a better idea of how visually-impaired users access information on a computer.

4 Click on the **VoiceOver** button to enable VoiceOver, which provides a spoken description of what is on the screen

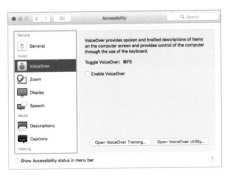

...cont'd

The **Audio**, **Keyboard** and **Mouse & Trackpad** accessibility options have links to additional options within their own System Preferences.

5 Click on the **Audio** button to select an on-screen flash for alerts, and how sound is played

6 Click on the **Keyboard** button to access options for customizing the keyboard

7 Click on the **Mouse & Trackpad** button to access options for customizing these devices

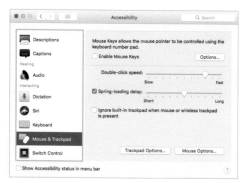

8 Click on the **Dictation** button to select options for using spoken commands

The Spoken Word

macOS High Sierra not only has numerous apps for adding text to documents, emails and messages; it also has a Dictation function so that you can speak what you want to appear on screen. To set up and use the Dictation feature:

1 Click on the **Dictation** tab in **System Preferences > Keyboard**

Dictation

2 Click on the **On** button to enable Dictation

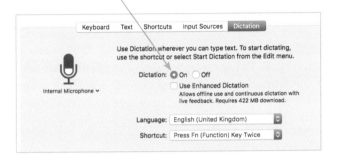

Hot tip

51

Punctuation can be added with the dictation function, by speaking commands such as "comma" or "question mark". These will then be converted into the appropriate symbols.

3 Click on the **Enable Dictation** button

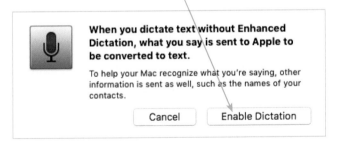

4 Once Dictation has been turned On, it can be accessed in relevant apps by selecting **Edit** > **Start Dictation** from the Menu bar

Start Dictation

5 Start talking when the microphone icon appears. Click **Done** when you have finished recording your text

When shutting down, make sure you have saved all of your open documents, although High Sierra will prompt you to do this if you have forgotten.

macOS High Sierra has a **Resume** function where your MacBook opens up in the same state as when you shut it down. See page 80 for details.

Shutting Down

The Apple menu (which can be accessed by clicking on the Apple icon at the top-left corner of the Desktop, or any subsequent macOS window) has been standardized in macOS. This means that it has the same options regardless of the app in which you are working. This has a number of advantages, not least being the fact that it makes it easier to shut down your MacBook. When shutting down, there are four options that can be selected:

- **Sleep**. This puts the MacBook into hibernation mode; i.e. the screen goes blank and the hard drive becomes inactive. This state is maintained until the mouse is moved or a key is pressed on the keyboard. This then wakes up the MacBook and it is ready to continue work. It is a good idea to add a login password for accessing the MacBook when it wakes up, otherwise other people could wake it up and gain access to it. To add a login password, go to **System Preferences > Security & Privacy** and click on the **General** tab. Check **On** the **Require password** checkbox and select from one of the timescale options (**immediately** is best).

- **Restart**. This closes down the MacBook and then restarts it again. This can be useful if you have added new software and your computer requires a restart to make it active.

- **Shut Down**. This closes down the MacBook completely once you have finished working.

- **Log Out**. This logs you out of your current session and closes down your open apps. You can then log back in without turning off your MacBook and return to your previously-open apps by using the **Resume** function; see tip.

4 Getting Up and Running

This chapter looks at some of the essential features of High Sierra. These include the Dock for organizing and accessing all of the elements of your MacBook, and items for arranging folders and files. It also covers Apple's online sharing service, iCloud, which can be used to back up a variety of content and also share items such as music, books, calendars and apps with up to six other family members.

The Dock is always displayed as a line of icons, but this can be orientated either vertically or horizontally (see next page).

Items on the Dock can be opened by clicking on them once, rather than having to double-click on them. Once they have been selected, the icon bobs up and down until the item is available.

Introducing the Dock

The Dock is one of the main organizational elements of macOS. Its main function is to help organize and access apps, folders and files. In addition, with its rich translucent colors and elegant graphical icons, it also makes an aesthetically-pleasing addition to the Desktop. The main things to remember about the Dock are:

- It is divided into two: apps go on the left of the dividing line; all other items go on the right.

- It can be customized in a number of ways.

By default, the Dock appears at the bottom of the screen:

Apps go here   Dividing line   Open items

If an app window is closed, the app remains open and the window is placed within the app icon on the Dock. If an item is minimized, it goes on the right of the Dock dividing line.

Setting Dock Preferences

As with most elements of macOS, the Dock can be modified in several ways. This can affect both the appearance of the Dock, and the way it operates. To set Dock preferences:

1 Select **System Preferences** > **Dock**

2 The Dock preferences allow you to change its size, orientation, the way icons appear with magnification, and effects for when items are minimized

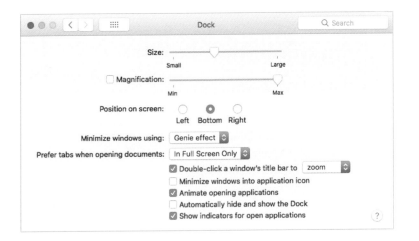

For instance, the size of the Dock can be reduced so that it only takes up a proportion of the width of the screen:

Hot tip

The Apple menu is constantly available in High Sierra, regardless of the app in which you are working. The menu options are also constant in all apps.

55

Don't forget

You will not be able to make the Dock size so large that some of the icons would not be visible on the Desktop. By default, the Dock is resized so that everything is always visible.

...cont'd

The **Position on screen** options enable you to place the Dock on the left, right or bottom of the screen:

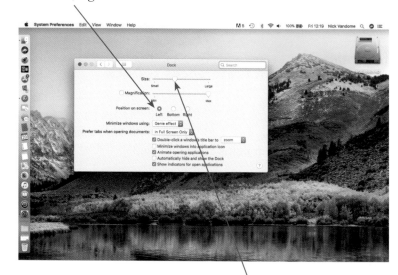

1 Drag the **Dock Size** slider to increase or decrease the size of the Dock

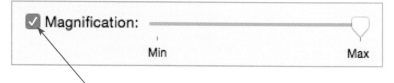

2 Check **On** the **Magnification** box and drag the slider to determine the size to which icons are enlarged when the cursor is moved over them

The effects that are applied to items when they are minimized is one of the features of macOS (it is not absolutely necessary but it sums up the Apple ethos of trying to enhance the user experience as much as possible).

The **Genie effect** shrinks the item to be minimized like a genie going back into its lamp:

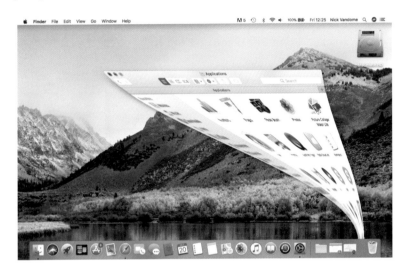

Open windows can also be minimized by double-clicking on their title bar (the thin bar at the top of the window, next to the three window buttons).

Manual resizing

In addition to changing the size of the Dock by using the Dock preferences dialog box, it can also be resized manually:

1 Drag vertically on the Dock dividing line to increase or decrease its size

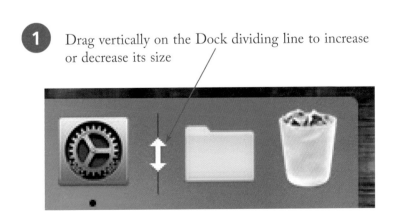

Stacks on the Dock

Stacking items

To save space, it is possible to add folders to the Dock, from where their contents can be accessed. This is known as Stacks. By default, a stack for downloaded files is created on the Dock. To use Stacks:

1 To create a new Stack, drag a folder onto the Dock. Stacked items are placed on the right of the Dock dividing line

2 Click on a Stack to view its contents

3 Stacks can be viewed as:

● A grid.

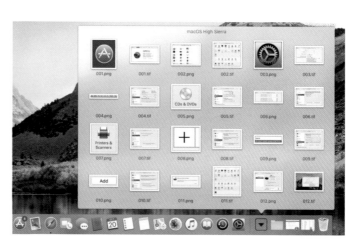

● A fan, depending on the number of items it contains.

Move the cursor over a Stack on the Dock and press Ctrl + click to access options for how that Stack is displayed.

● A list. Click on a folder to view its contents within a Stack, then click on files to open them in their relevant app.

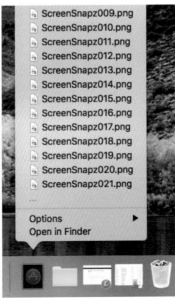

Any new items that are added to the folder will also be visible through the Stack.

Dock Menus

One of the features of the Dock is that it can display contextual menus for selected items. This means that it shows menus with options that are applicable to the item that is being accessed. This can only be done when an item has been opened.

Click on **Quit** on the Dock's contextual menu to close an open app or file, depending on which side of the dividing bar the item is located.

1 Click and hold on the black dot below an app's icon to display an item's individual context menu

2 Click on **Options**, then **Show in Finder** to see where the item is located on your computer

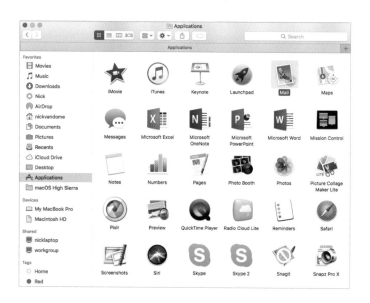

Working with Dock Items

Adding items

As many items as you like can be added to the Dock; the only restriction is the size of monitor in which to display all of the Dock items (the size of the Dock can be reduced to accommodate more icons, but you have to be careful that all of the icons are still legible). To add items to the Dock:

1 Locate the required item in the Finder and drag it onto the Dock. All of the other icons move along to make space for the new one

Don't forget

Icons on the Dock are shortcuts to the related item rather than the item itself, which remains in its original location.

Keep in Dock

Every time you open a new app, its icon will appear in the Dock for the duration that the app is open, even if it has not previously been put in the Dock. If you then decide that you would like to keep it in the Dock, you can do so as follows:

1 Click and hold on the black dot below an open app

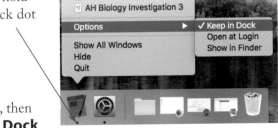

2 Click on **Options**, then **Keep in Dock** to ensure the app remains in the Dock when it is closed

...cont'd

Removing items

Any item, except the Finder, can be removed from the Dock. However, this does not remove it from your computer; it just removes the shortcut for accessing it. You will still be able to locate it in its folder in the Finder and, if required, drag it back onto the Dock. To remove items from the Dock:

Hot tip

When an icon is dragged from the Dock, it has to be moved a reasonable distance before the Remove alert appears.

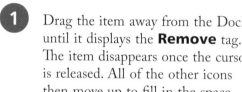

1 Drag the item away from the Dock until it displays the **Remove** tag. The item disappears once the cursor is released. All of the other icons then move up to fill in the space

Removing open apps

You can remove an app from the Dock, even if it is open and running. To do this:

Don't forget

If **Keep in Dock** has been selected for an item (see previous page) the app will remain in the Dock even when it has been closed.

1 Drag an app off the Dock while it is running. Initially, the icon will remain on the Dock because the app is still open

2 When the app is closed (click and hold on the dot underneath the item and select **Quit**) its icon will be removed from the Dock

Trash

The Trash folder is a location for placing items that you do not need anymore. However, when items are placed in the Trash, they are not removed from your computer. This requires another command, as the Trash is really a holding area before you decide you want to remove items permanently. The Trash can also be used for ejecting removable disks attached to your MacBook.

Sending items to the Trash
Items can be sent to the Trash by dragging them from the location in which they are stored:

1 Drag an item over the **Trash** icon to place it in the Trash folder

2 Click once on the **Trash** icon on the Dock to view its contents

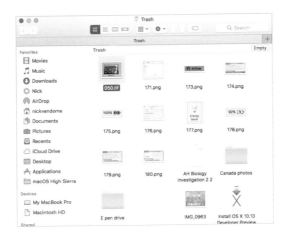

Items can also be sent to the Trash by selecting them and then selecting **File** > **Move to Trash** from the Menu bar.

All of the items within the Trash can be removed in a single command: Select **Finder** > **Empty Trash** from the Menu bar to remove all of the items in the Trash folder.

About iCloud

Cloud computing is an attractive proposition, and one that has gained greatly in popularity in recent years. As a concept, it consists of storing your content on an external computer server. This not only gives you added security in terms of backing up your information; it also means that the content can then be shared over a variety of devices.

iCloud is Apple's consumer cloud computing product that consists of online services such as email; a calendar; contacts; and saving documents. iCloud provides users with a way to save their files and content to the online service, and then use them across their Apple devices such as other Mac computers, iPhones, iPads and iPod Touches.

About iCloud

iCloud can be set up from this icon within System Preferences:

You can use iCloud to save and share the following:

- Photos
- Mail and Safari settings
- Documents
- Backups
- Notes
- Reminders
- Contacts and Calendars

When you save an item to the iCloud, it automatically pushes it to all of your other compatible devices. You do not have to manually sync anything; iCloud does it all for you.

The standard iCloud service is free, and this includes an iCloud email address and 5GB of online storage (*at the time of printing*).

There is also a version of iCloud for Windows, which can be accessed for download from the Apple website at www.apple.com/icloud/setup/pc.html

Setting up iCloud

To use iCloud with High Sierra you need to first have an Apple ID. This is a service you can register for to be able to access a range of Apple facilities, including iCloud. You can register with an email address and a password. When you first start using iCloud you will be prompted for your Apple ID details. If you do not have an Apple ID you can create one at this point:

1 Sign in with your Apple ID, or

2 Click on the **Create Apple ID...** button and follow the steps to create your Apple ID

When you have an Apple ID and an iCloud account, you can also use the iCloud website to access your content. Access the website at www.icloud.com and log in with your Apple ID details.

65

Setting up iCloud
To use iCloud:

1 Open **System Preferences** and click on the **iCloud** button

2 Check on the items you want included within iCloud. All of these items will be backed up and shared across all of your Apple devices

The online iCloud service includes your online email service; Contacts; Calendar; Reminders; Notes; and versions of Pages, Keynote and Numbers. You can log in to your iCloud account from any internet-enabled device.

About the iCloud Drive

One of the options in the iCloud section is for the iCloud Drive. This can be used to store documents and other content so that you can use them on any other Apple devices that you have, such as an iPhone or an iPad. With iCloud Drive you can start work on a document on one device and continue on another device from where you left off. To set up the iCloud Drive:

1 Click on the **iCloud** button in **System Preferences**

iCloud

Beware

If the **Desktop & Documents Folders** option is selected for the iCloud Drive, this can take up a lot of iCloud storage as all items in these locations will be saved to the iCloud Drive, which counts towards your iCloud storage limit.

2 Check **On** the **iCloud Drive** option and click on the **Options...** button

☑ iCloud Drive   Options...

3 Select the apps that you want to use with the iCloud Drive

Documents | Look Me Up By Email

Apps that store documents and data in iCloud will appear here:

☐ Desktop & Documents Folders

☑ Automator

☑ Preview

☑ QuickTime Player

☑ Script Editor

☑ TextEdit

☑ Optimize Mac Storage

The full contents of iCloud Drive will be stored on this Mac if you have enough space. Older Documents will be stored only in iCloud when space is needed.

Done

Don't forget

Pages is the Apple app for word processing; Numbers for spreadsheets; and Keynote for presentations. These can all be used to save files into the iCloud Drive.

4 Click on the **Done** button

...cont'd

Using the iCloud Drive
To work with files in the iCloud Drive:

1 In the Finder sidebar click on the **iCloud Drive** button

2 Certain iCloud Drive folders are already created, based on the apps that you have selected on the previous page. These are the default folders into which content from their respective apps will be placed (although others can also be selected, if required). Double-click on a folder to view its contents

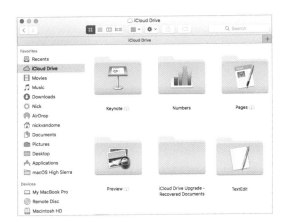

Hot tip

Another useful iCloud function is the iCloud Keychain (see pages 76-79 for details).

67

3 To save files into an iCloud Drive folder, select **File > Save As** (or **Save**) from the Menu bar, click on the **iCloud Drive** button in the Finder sidebar, and navigate to the required folder for the file

Continuity

One of the main themes of macOS High Sierra, and iOS for mobile devices (iOS 8 and later), is to make all of your content available on all of your Apple devices. This is known as Continuity: when you create something on one device you can then pick it up and finish it on another. This is done through iCloud. To do this:

1 Ensure the app has iCloud activated, as on page 65

2 Create the content in the app on your MacBook

3 Open the same app on another Apple device; e.g. an iPad. The item created on your MacBook should be available to view and edit. Any changes will then show up on the file on your MacBook too

Hot tip

It is also possible to continue an email with the Continuity feature. First create it on your MacBook and then close it. You will be prompted to save the email as a draft and, if you do this, you will be able to open it from the **Drafts** mailbox on another Apple device.

Handoff

Handoff is one of the key features of Continuity, and it displays icons of items that you have opened on another device, such as Safari web pages. Handoff does not work with all devices, and it only works if both devices have OS X Yosemite (or later) and iOS 8 (or later), for mobile devices.

To use Handoff you will need to do the following:

- Your MacBook must be running OS X Yosemite (or later) and your mobile device (iPhone 5 and later, iPad 4th generation and later, all models of iPad mini and the 5th generation iPod Touch) must have iOS 8 (or later).

- Your MacBook has to support Bluetooth 4.0, which means that most pre-2012 Macs are not compatible with Handoff.

To check if your MacBook supports Handoff:

1 Select **Apple menu** > **About This Mac** > **System Report**. Click on **Bluetooth** to see if Handoff is supported

Bluetooth Low Energy Supported:	Yes
Handoff Supported:	Yes
Instant Hotspot Supported:	Yes

2 Turn on Bluetooth on your MacBook (in **System Preferences**) and on your mobile device (in **Settings**)

3 Turn on Handoff on your MacBook (**System Preferences** > **General** and check on **Allow Handoff Between this Mac and your iCloud Devices**) and on your mobile device (**Settings** > **General** > **Handoff**)

4 When Handoff is activated, compatible apps will be displayed at the left-hand side of the Dock when they have been opened on another device

The apps that work with Handoff are Mail, Safari, Maps, Messages, Reminders, Calendar, Contacts, Notes, Pages, Numbers and Keynote.

If Handoff is not working, try turning both devices off and on, and do the same with Bluetooth. Also, try logging out of, and then back in to, your iCloud account on both devices.

About Family Sharing

As everyone gets more and more digital devices it is becoming increasingly important to be able to share content with other people, particularly family members. In macOS High Sierra, and iCloud, the Family Sharing function enables you to share items that you have downloaded from the App Store, such as music and movies, with up to six other family members, as long as they have an Apple ID. Once this has been set up it is also possible to share items such as family calendars and photos, and even see where family members' devices are located. To set up Family Sharing:

Don't forget

To use Family Sharing, other family members must have an Apple device using either iOS 8 (or later) for a mobile device (iPad, iPhone or iPod Touch) or OS X Yosemite (or later) for a desktop or laptop Mac computer.

1 Click on the **iCloud** button in **System Preferences**

iCloud

2 Click on the **Set Up Family** (here the **Manage Family** button appears, since Family Sharing has already been set up). Click on **Get Started** and then click on the **Continue** button

3 One person will be the organizer of Family Sharing – i.e. in charge of it – and if you set it up then it will be you. Click on the **+** button to add other family members

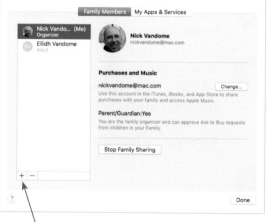

4 Enter the name or email address of a

family member and click on the **Continue** button

5 Verify your debit or credit card information for your iCloud

account, as this will be used by the family member for making purchases. Click on the **Continue** button

6 Enter your Apple ID password and click on the **Continue** button

7 An invitation is sent to the selected person. They have to accept this before they can participate in Family Sharing

If children are part of the Family Sharing group you can specify that they need your permission before downloading any items from the iTunes Store, the App Store or the iBooks Store. To do this, click on **iCloud** in **System Preferences** and click on the **Manage Family** button. Select a family member and check **On** the **Ask to Buy** button. You will then receive a notification whenever they want to buy something, and you can either allow or deny their request.

Using Family Sharing

Once Family Sharing has been set up it can be used by members of the groups to share music, apps, movies and books. There is also a shared Family calendar that can be used, and it is also possible to view the location of the devices of the family members.

Sharing music

To share music and other content from the iTunes Store, such as movies and TV shows:

1 Click on the **iTunes** app on the Dock

2 Click on the **Store** button and click on the **Purchased** link

3 By default, your own purchases are displayed. Click on the name to the right of the **Purchased** button to view other members of Family Sharing

4 Click on another family member to view their purchases (they will be able to do this for your purchases too)

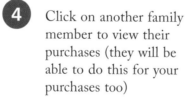

5 Click on the iCloud button to download the other family member's music tracks or albums

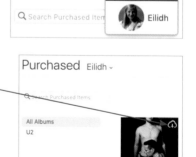

Hot tip

You have to be connected to the internet and be online to access the iTunes Store and view purchases from other family members. When you do this, you can play their songs without having to download them. However, if you want to be able to use them when you are offline, then you will have to download them first, as in Step 5.

Sharing apps

Apps can also be shared from the App Store. To do this:

1 Click on the **App Store** app on the Dock

2 Click on the **Purchased** button

3 By default, your own purchases are displayed. Click on the **My Purchases** button to view other members of Family Sharing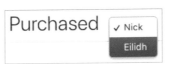

4 Click on another family member to view and download their purchased apps (they will be able to do this for your apps too)

Sharing books

Books can also be shared in a similar way to items from the iTunes Store and the App Store. To do this:

1 Click on the **iBooks** app on the Dock

2 Click on the **iBooks Store** button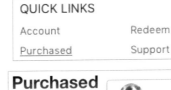

3 Click on the **Purchased** link, under the **Quick Links** heading

QUICK LINKS

Account   Redeem
Purchased   Support

4 By default, your own purchases are displayed. Click on the name to the right of the **Purchased** button to view other members of Family Sharing and any books they have downloaded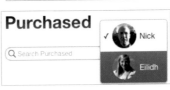

Don't forget

More than one family member can use content in the Family Sharing group at the same time.

...cont'd

Sharing calendars

Family Sharing also generates a Family calendar that can be used by all Family Sharing members:

Don't forget

Other members of the Family Sharing group can add items to the Family calendar and, when they do, you will be sent a notification that appears on your MacBook.

Hot tip

To change the color of a calendar, click on the **Calendars** button at the top left of the window. Ctrl + click on a calendar name, and select a color from the bottom of the panel, or click on **Custom Color...** to choose from the full spectrum.

1 Open the **Calendar** app

2 Ctrl + click on a date to create a **New Event**. The current calendar (shown in the top right-hand corner) will probably not be the Family one. Click on this button to change the calendar

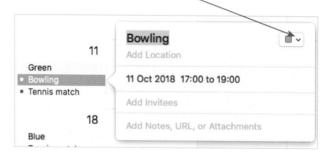

3 Click on the **Family** calendar

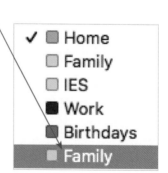

4 Complete the details for the event. It will be added to your calendar, with the Family color tag. Other people in your
Family Sharing circle will have this event added to their Family calendar too, and they will be sent a notification

Finding lost family devices

Family Sharing also makes it possible to see where everyone's devices are, which can be useful for locating people, but particularly if a device belonging to a Family Sharing member is lost or stolen. To do this:

1 Ensure that the **Find My Mac** function is turned on in the **iCloud** System Preferences, and log in to your online iCloud account at **www.icloud.com**

2 Click on the **Find iPhone** button (this works for other Apple devices too)

3 Devices that are turned on, online and with iCloud activated are shown by green dots

The locations of devices are shown on a map, and you can zoom in on the map to see their locations more accurately.

4 Click on a green dot to display information about the device. Click on the **i** symbol to access options for managing the device remotely

Always have Find My Mac turned on in case your Mac is lost or stolen and you need to locate it.

5 There are options to send an alert sound to the device, lock it remotely or erase its contents (if you are concerned about it having fallen into the wrong hands)

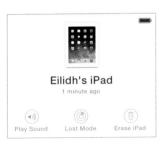

iCloud Keychain

One of the big issues of online activity is remembering passwords on websites, and also ensuring that they are as secure as possible. This is made all the more significant if you are using different devices to access websites.

On Mac computers and iOS 8 (and later) mobile devices, password management and security is handled through the iCloud Keychain function, using Safari as your web browser. This can be used to save passwords and credit card information when you enter them into websites, and also generate new, secure, passwords if required. This information is stored in the iCloud, and so is available on all of the compatible Apple devices on which you are accessing the web with Safari. To set up iCloud Keychain:

Don't forget

You must have an Apple ID and have iCloud turned on in order to use the iCloud Keychain functionality.

1 Click on the **iCloud** button in **System Preferences**

iCloud

2 In the iCloud window, click on the **Keychain** checkbox

3 Enter your **Apple ID** password to set up iCloud Keychain. Click on the **OK** button

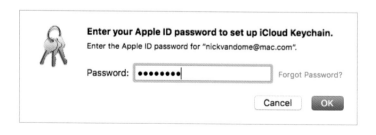

Enter your Apple ID password to set up iCloud Keychain.
Enter the Apple ID password for "nickvandome@mac.com".

Password: •••••••

Forgot Password?

Cancel   OK

4 Enter a security code for iCloud Keychain, then click on the **Next** button

5 If it is the first time you have set up iCloud Keychain, you will be sent a verification code to the mobile/cell number that you have linked to your Apple ID

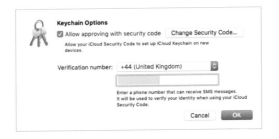

Don't forget

When iCloud Keychain is first set up, the iCloud Security Code is created for the first time in Step 4. This can be used subsequently to make any changes to your iCloud Keychain settings.

6 If you have set up iCloud Keychain on another Apple device, you can request approval from that device, which will then provide the Keychain details that it has stored. Click on the **Request Approval** button

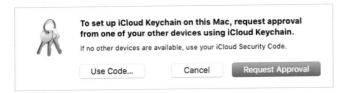

Beware

Make sure that you have the correct mobile/cell number registered with your Apple ID, so that you can receive the verification code in Step 5, if required.

7 Click on the **OK** button and confirm the approval on the other device

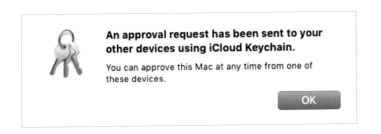

Using iCloud Keychain

Once iCloud Keychain has been set up, it can be used to remember passwords and credit card information on websites and ensure this information is available across all of your compatible Apple devices. Passwords can also be autofilled so that you do not have to enter them each time. This can be set up within the Preferences of the Safari browser app. To do this:

1 Open Safari and select **Safari > Preferences** from the Menu bar

2 Click on the **Passwords** tab and check **On** the **AutoFill user names and passwords** checkbox

If AutoFill is turned on, and iCloud Keychain is being used, Safari will remember usernames and passwords and pre-insert them whenever you visit a website that has been set up for this.

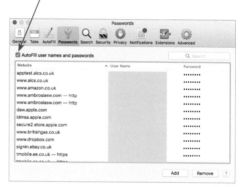

3 Click on the **AutoFill** tab and select the items that you want to be included for AutoFill

4 When you first enter an existing password into a website, you will be prompted to save it in iCloud Keychain. Click on the **Save Password** button to do this

5 Once AutoFill has been activated, when you start to fill in the username and password on a website that has been used before, you will be prompted to fill the fields from the AutoFill information

6 For a website on which you have not created a user account and password, you will be prompted by iCloud Keychain to use the Safari suggested one

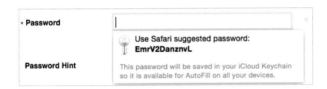

Although the passwords created by iCloud Keychain are generally more secure than the ones created by individuals, they are not always considered the most secure in terms of internet security. However, for most purposes they will provide a good level of online security.

Keychain settings
Some of the Keychain settings can be changed within iCloud System Preferences:

1 Click on the Keychain **Options...** button

2 Make any changes to the options, as required. These include allowing approval for your iCloud Security Code to be used to set up Keychain on other devices, and also the phone number needed for verification purposes

Resuming

One of the chores of computing is that when you close down your computer you have to first close down all of your open documents and apps, and then open them all again when you turn your machine back on again. However, macOS has a feature that allows you to continue working exactly where you left off, even if you turn off your computer. To do this:

1 Before you close down, all of your open documents and apps will be available

2 Select the **Shut Down...** or **Restart...** option from the Apple menu

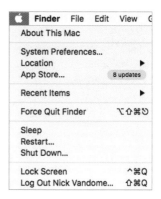

3 Make sure this box is checked **On** (this will ensure that all of your items will appear as before, once the MacBook is closed down and then opened again)

4 Confirm the **Shut Down** or **Restart** command

5 Finder

The principal way of moving around High Sierra is the Finder. This enables you to access items and organize your apps, folders and files. This chapter looks at how to use the Finder and get the most out of this powerful tool for navigating around High Sierra. It covers how to customize the interface, numerous options for working with folders and files, and also sharing items with other apps directly from the Finder.

Working with the Finder

If you were only able to use one item on the Dock, it would be the Finder. This is the gateway to all of the elements of your MacBook. It is possible to get to selected items through other routes, but the Finder is the only location where you can gain access to everything on your system. If you ever feel that you are getting lost within macOS, click on the Finder and then you should begin to feel more at home. To access the Finder:

 Click once on this icon on the Dock

Overview

The Finder has its own toolbar; a sidebar from which items can be accessed; and a main window where the contents of selected items can be viewed:

Forward and back   View options   Actions button   Search

View recent files

Folders are displayed here

Sidebar

Tags

Main window

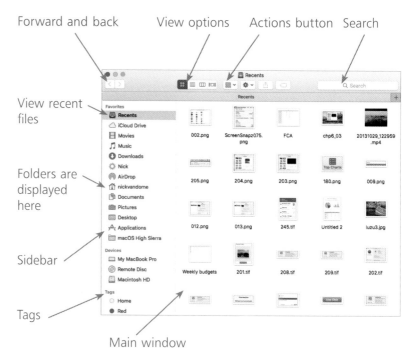

Don't forget

A link to the iCloud Drive is also included in the Finder sidebar.

Don't forget

The **Actions** button has options for displaying information about a selected item, and also options for how it is displayed within the Finder.

Finder Folders

Recents

This contains all of the latest files on which you have been working. They are sorted into categories according to file type so that you can search through them quickly. This is an excellent way to locate items without having to look through a lot of folders. To access this:

1 Click on this link in the Finder sidebar to access the contents of your **Recents** folder

2 All of your recent files are displayed in individual categories. Click on the headings at the top of each category to sort items by those criteria

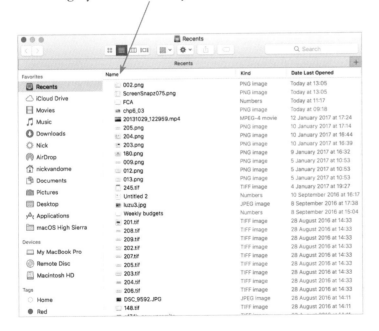

3 Double-click on an item to open it from the Finder

The Finder is always open (as denoted by the black dot graphic underneath its icon on the Dock) and it cannot readily be closed down or removed.

The Finder sidebar has the macOS High Sierra transparency feature, so that you can see some of the open window or Desktop behind it.

To change the display of folders in the sidebar, click on the **Finder** menu on the top toolbar. Select **Preferences...** and click on the **Sidebar** tab. Under **Show these items in the sidebar:**, select the items you want included.

...cont'd

Home folder

This contains the contents of your own Home directory, containing your personal folders and files. macOS inserts some pre-named folders that it thinks will be useful, but it is possible to rename, rearrange or delete these as you please. It is also possible to add as many more folders as you want.

1 Click on your Apple ID account name in the sidebar to access the contents of your **Home** folder

2 The Home folder contains the **Public** folder that can be used to share files with other users if the computer is part of a network

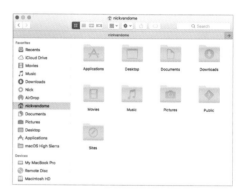

Applications

This folder contains all of the applications on your MacBook. They can also be accessed from the Launchpad, as shown on pages 118-119.

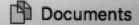

Downloads

This is the default folder for any files or apps that you download (other than those from the Mac App Store).

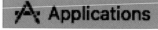

Documents

This is part of your Home folder but is put on the Finder sidebar for ease of access. New folders can be created for different types of documents.

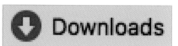

Hot tip

When you are creating documents, macOS by default recognizes their type and then, when you save them, suggests the most applicable folder in your Home directory in which to save them. So, if you have created a word processed document, High Sierra will suggest you save it in Documents; if it is a photograph it will suggest Pictures; if it is a video it will suggest Movies; and so on.

84

Finder Views

The way in which items are displayed within the Finder can be amended in a variety of ways, depending on how you want to view the contents of a folder. Different folders can have their own viewing options applied to them, and these will stay in place until a new option is specified.

Icon view

One of the viewing options for displaying items within the Finder is as Icons. This provides a graphical representation of the items in the Finder. It is possible to customize Icon view:

Use the Back and Forward buttons at the top of the Finder to move between windows that you have previously visited.

1 Click here on the Finder toolbar to access **Icon** view

2 Select **View** from the Menu bar, check on **as Icons** and select **Show View Options** to access the options for customizing Icon view

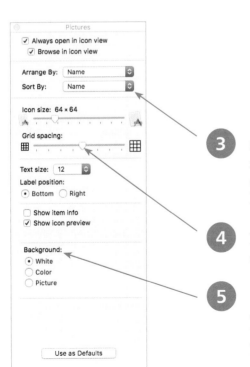

The **Arrange By** options can be used to arrange icons into specific groups; e.g. by name or type, or to snap them to an invisible grid so that they have an ordered appearance.

3 Select an option for the way icons are arranged in Finder windows

4 Drag this slider to set the icon size

A very large icon size can be useful for people with poor eyesight, but it does take up a lot more space in a window.

5 Select an option for the background of the Finder window

...cont'd

List view

List view can be used to show the items within a Finder window as a list, with additional information shown next to them. This can be a more efficient method than Icon view if there are a lot of items within a folder: List view enables you to see more items at one time and also view the additional information.

Don't forget

List view can be customized to include a variety of information such as file size and date last modified.

 Click here on the Finder toolbar to access **List** view

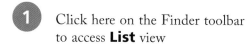

2 The name of each folder or file is displayed here. If any item has additional elements within it, this is represented by a small triangle next to it. Additional information in List view, such as file size and last modified date, is included in columns to the right

Column view

Column view is a useful option if you want to trace the location of a particular item; i.e. see the full path of its location, starting from the hard drive.

1 Click here on the Finder toolbar to access **Column** view

2 Click on an item to see everything within that folder. If an arrow follows an item it means that there are further items to view

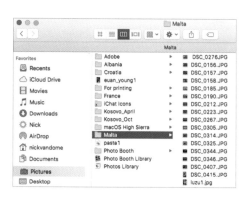

Covers and Quick Look

Covers

Covers is a feature on the MacBook that enables you to view items as large icons. To use Covers:

1 Select a folder and at the top of the Finder window click on this button

2 The items within the folder are displayed in their cover state

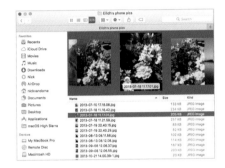

3 Drag each item to view the next one. You can also move between items by swiping left or right on a trackpad

Quick Look

Through a Finder option called Quick Look, it is possible to view the content of a file without having to first open it. To do this:

1 Select a file within the Finder

> DSC_0327.JPG
> DSC_0328.jpg
> DSC_0329.JPG
> DSC_0330.JPG
> DSC_0331.JPG

2 Press the space bar

3 The contents of the file are displayed without it opening in its default app

4 Click on the cross to close Quick Look

Hot tip

In Quick Look it is even possible to preview videos or presentations without having to first open them in their default app.

Finder Toolbar

Customizing the toolbar

As with most elements of macOS, it is possible to customize the Finder toolbar:

1 Select **View** > **Customize Toolbar...** from the Menu bar

2 Drag items from the window into the toolbar

3 Alternatively, drag the default set of icons into the toolbar

4 Click **Done** at the bottom of the window

Finder Sidebar

Using the sidebar

The sidebar is the left-hand panel of the Finder, which can be used to access items on your MacBook:

1 Click on a button on the sidebar

2 Its contents are displayed in the main Finder window

Adding to the sidebar

Items that you access most frequently can be added to the sidebar. To do this:

1 Drag an item from the main Finder window onto the sidebar. A line appears, determining the location

2 The item is added to the sidebar. You can do this with apps, folders and files

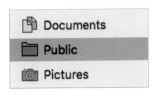

When items are added to the Finder sidebar a shortcut, or alias, is inserted into the sidebar, not the actual item.

Items can be removed from the sidebar by Ctrl + clicking on them and selecting **Remove from Sidebar** from the contextual menu.

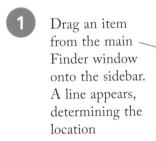

Finder Tabs

Tabs in web browsers are now well established, where you can have several pages open within the same browser window. This technology is utilized in the Finder in macOS High Sierra with the use of Finder Tabs. This enables different folders to be open in different tabs within the Finder, so that you can organize your content exactly how you want. To do this:

Hot tip

In macOS High Sierra, tabs are available in a range of apps that open multiple windows, including the Apple productivity apps: Pages, Numbers and Keynote. If the tabs are not showing, select **View** > **Show Tab Bar** from the app's Menu bar.

1 Select **View** > **Show Tab Bar** from the Finder Menu bar

2 Click on this button to add a new tab

3 At this point the content in the new tab is displayed for the window (see "Don't forget" tip)

Don't forget

To specify an option for what appears as the default for a new Finder window, click on the **Finder** menu and click on **Preferences**, then the **General** tab. Under **New Finder windows show:**, select the default window to be used.

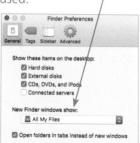

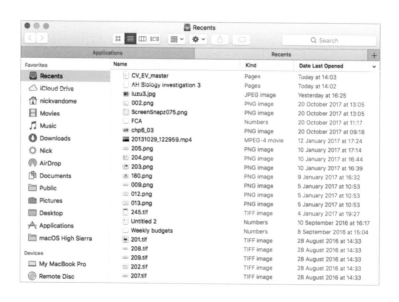

4 Each tab view can be customized, and this is independent of the other tabs

Finder Tags

When creating content in macOS High Sierra you may find that you have documents of different types that cover the same topic. For instance, you may have work-related documents in Pages for reports, Keynote for presentations and Numbers for spreadsheets. With the Finder Tags function it is possible to link related content items through the use of colored tags. These can be added to items in the Finder and also in apps when content is created.

Tags can also be added to items by Ctrl + clicking on them and selecting the required tag from the menu that appears. Alternatively, they can be added from this button on the main Finder toolbar.

1 The tags are listed in the Finder sidebar. (If you can't see the list, hover the cursor over the Tags heading and then click on the **Show** button)

2 To give tags specific names, Ctrl + click on one and click on the **Rename** link

3 To add tags, select the required items in the Finder window

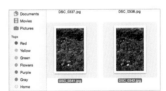

Tags can also be added when documents are created in certain apps, such as Pages, Keynote and Numbers: select **File** > **Save**, click in the **Tags** box and select the required tag. Click on the **Save** button.

4 Drag the selected items over the appropriate tag

5 The tags are added to the selected items

Searching with the Finder

On MacBooks it is possible to search your folders and files, using the Finder (in addition to Spotlight search and using Siri).

Hot tip

When entering search keywords try to be as specific as possible. This will cut down on the number of unwanted results.

Don't forget

Both folders and files will be displayed in the Finder as part of the search results.

1 In the Finder window, enter the search keyword(s) in this box and select the search criteria. The results are shown in the Finder

2 Select the areas over which you want the search performed; e.g. Home folder or Pictures (if a folder is selected in the Finder sidebar, this will be available as an option to search over)

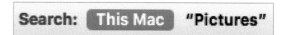

3 Double-click on a file to open it or, if there are folders in the search results, double-click on one to open it and view its contents

Copying and Moving Items

Items can be copied and moved within macOS by using the copy and paste method, or by dragging.

Copy and paste

1 Select an item (or items) and select **Edit > Copy Item(s)** from the Menu bar

Edit	View	Go	Window	He
Undo Move of "IES"				⌘Z
Redo				⇧⌘Z
Cut				⌘X
Copy 5 Items				**⌘C**
Paste				⌘V
Select All				⌘A
Show Clipboard				
Start Dictation				fn fn
Emoji & Symbols				^⌘Space

2 Move to the target location and select **Edit > Paste Item(s)** from the Menu bar. The item is then pasted into the new location

Edit	View	Go	Window	He
Undo Move of "IES"				⌘Z
Redo				⇧⌘Z
Cut				⌘X
Copy				⌘C
Paste 5 Items				**⌘V**
Select All				⌘A
Show Clipboard				
Start Dictation				fn fn
Emoji & Symbols				^⌘Space

Dragging

Drag a file from one location to another to move it to that location. (This requires two or more Finder windows to be open, or drag the item over a folder on the sidebar.)

Don't forget

When an item is copied, it is placed on the Clipboard and remains there until another item is copied.

Hot tip

macOS High Sierra supports the Universal Clipboard, where items can be copied on a device such as an iPhone and then pasted directly into a document on a Mac running macOS High Sierra. The mobile device has to be running iOS 10 (or later), and the Mac has to support the Universal Clipboard. The process is the same as regular copy and paste, except that each operation is performed on the separate devices and each app used has to be set up for iCloud. Also, Bluetooth and Wi-Fi have to be activated on both devices.

Working with Folders

When macOS High Sierra is installed, there are various folders that have already been created to hold apps and files. Some of these are essential (i.e. those containing apps), while others are created as an aid for where you might want to store the files that you create (such as the Pictures and Movies folders). Once you start working with macOS High Sierra you will probably want to create your own folders in which to store and organize your documents. This can be done on the Desktop or within any level of your existing folder structure. To create a new folder:

Folders are always denoted by a folder icon. This is the same regardless of the Finder view that is selected. The only difference is that the icon is larger in Icon view than in List or Column views.

1 Access the location in which you want to create the new folder (e.g. your Home folder) and select **File** > **New Folder** from the Menu bar

2 A new, empty folder is inserted at the selected location (named "untitled folder")

You can create as many "nested" folders (i.e. folders within other folders) as you want. However, this makes your folder structure more complicated and, after a time, you may forget where all your folders are and what they contain.

3 Overtype the file name with a new one. Press **Enter** on the keyboard

untitled folder

In Easy Steps

4 Double-click on a folder to view its contents (at this point it should be empty)

Content can be added to an empty folder by dragging it from another folder and dropping it into the new one.

Spring-loaded Folders

Another method for moving items with the Finder is to use the spring-loaded folder option. This enables you to drag items into a folder and then view the contents of the folder before you drop the item into it. This means that you can drag items into nested folders in a single operation. To do this:

1 Select the item you want to move

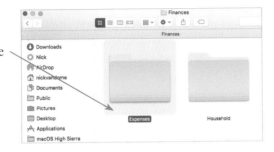

2 Drag the selected item over the folder into which you want to place it. Keep the trackpad held down

3 The folder will open, revealing its contents. The selected item can either be dropped into the folder or, if there are sub-folders, the same

operation can be repeated until you find the folder into which you want to place the selected item

Hot tip

The spring-loaded folder technique can be used to move items between different locations within the Finder; e.g. for moving files from your Pictures folder into your Home folder.

Beware

Do not release the trackpad until you have reached the location into which you want to place the selected item.

Smart Folders

When working on any computer it is inevitable that you will soon have a number of related files in different locations. This could be because you save your images in one folder, your word processing documents in another, web pages in another, and so on. This can cause difficulties when you are trying to keep track of a lot of related documents. macOS High Sierra overcomes this problem through the use of Smart Folders. These are folders that you set up using Finder search results as the foundation. Then, when new items are created that meet the original criteria, they are automatically included within the Smart Folder. To create a Smart Folder:

Numerous different Smart Folders can be created, for different types of files and information.

96

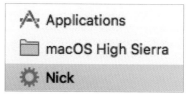

If you set very precise criteria for a Smart Folder this will result in a smaller number of items being included within it.

1 Conduct a search with the Finder search box

2 Once the search is completed, click the **Save** button to create a Smart Folder

3 Enter a name for the new Smart Folder and click on the **Save** button

4 The Smart Folder is added to the Finder sidebar. Click the Smart Folder to view its contents

Selecting Items

Apps and files within macOS folders can be selected by a variety of different methods:

Selecting by dragging
Click and drag the cursor to encompass the items to be selected. The selected items will become highlighted.

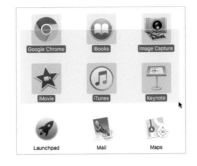

Selecting by clicking
Click once on an item to select it, hold down Shift and then click on another item in a list to select a consecutive group of items.

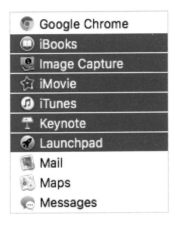

To select a non-consecutive group, select the first item by clicking on it once, then hold down the Command key (**cmd**) and select the other required items. The selected items will appear highlighted.

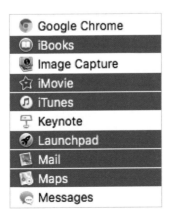

Select All
To select all of the items in a folder, select **Edit** > **Select All** from the Menu bar.

Once items have been selected, a single command can be applied to all of them. For instance, you can copy a group of items by selecting them and then applying the **Copy** command from the Menu bar.

To select all of the items in a folder, select **Edit** > **Select All** from the Menu bar. The Select All command selects all of the elements within the active item. For instance, if the active item is a word processing document, the Select All command will select all of the items within the document; if it is a folder, it will select all of the items within that folder. You can also click **cmd** + **A** to select all items.

Actions Button

The Finder Actions button provides a variety of options for any item, or items, selected in the Finder. To use this:

Don't forget

The icons on the Finder toolbar can be changed by customizing them – see page 88.

Hot tip

If an image in the **Pictures** folder has been selected, the Actions button can be used to set it as the Desktop picture, by selecting **Set Desktop Picture** at the bottom of the Actions menu.

Don't forget

The Actions button can also be used for labeling items. To do this, select the required items in the Finder and click on the colored buttons at the bottom of the Actions button menu. The selected color will be applied to the item names in the Finder.

1. Select an item, or group of items, about which you want to find out additional information

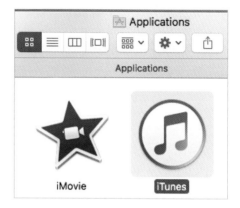

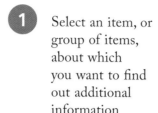

2. Click on the **Actions** button on the Finder toolbar

3. The available options for the selected item, or items, are displayed. These include **Get Info**, which displays additional information about an item such as file type, file size, creation and modification dates, and the default app for opening the item(s)

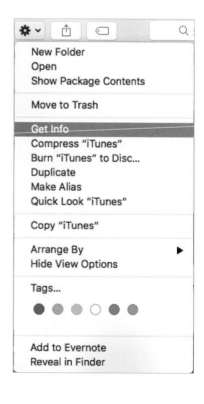

Sharing from the Finder

Also on the Finder toolbar is the Share button. This can be used to share a selected item, or items, in a variety of ways appropriate to the type of file that has been selected. For instance, a photo will have options including the photo-sharing site Flickr, while a text document will have fewer options. To share items directly from the Finder:

1. Locate and select the item(s) that you want to share

2. Click on the **Share** button on the Finder toolbar and select one of the options

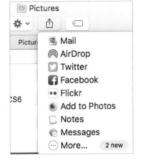

3. For some of the options, such as Twitter and Flickr, you will be asked to add an account. If you already have an account with these services you can enter the details or, if not, you can create a new account

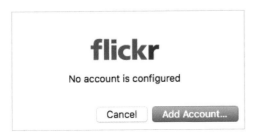

Hot tip

The Share button is available in many apps throughout macOS. This means that there is increased functionality for sharing items. For instance, you can share web pages from Safari or share photos from the Photos app.

Don't forget

This button on the Finder toolbar is a button for changing the arrangement of items within the Finder. Click on this button to access arrangement options such as Name, Date and Size.

Hot tip

You can also add your social networking accounts from **System Preferences** > **Internet Accounts**. Select the required account and enter your login details.

Menus

The main Apple Menu bar in macOS High Sierra contains a variety of menus, which are accessed when the Finder is the active window. When individual apps are open they have their own menu bars, although in a lot of cases these are similar to the standard Menu bar, particularly for the built-in macOS High Sierra apps such as Calendar, Contacts and Notes.

- **Apple menu**. This is denoted by a translucent gray apple and contains general information about the computer, a preferences option for changing the functionality and appearance of your MacBook, and options for closing down the computer.

- **Finder menu**. This contains preference options for amending the functionality and appearance of the Finder, and also options for emptying the Trash and accessing other apps (under the Services option).

- **File menu**. This contains common commands for working with open documents, such as opening and closing files, creating aliases, moving to the Trash, ejecting external devices, and burning discs.

- **Edit menu**. This contains common commands that apply to the majority of apps used on the MacBook. These include Undo, Cut, Copy, Paste, Select All and Show the contents of the Clipboard; i.e. items that have been cut or copied.

- **View menu**. This contains options for how windows and folders are displayed within the Finder and for customizing the Finder toolbar. This includes showing or hiding the Finder sidebar, and selecting view options for the size at which icons are displayed within Finder windows.

- **Go menu**. This can be used to navigate around your computer. This includes moving to your Recents folder, your Home folder, your Applications folder, and recently-accessed folders.

- **Window menu**. This contains commands to organize the currently-open apps and files on your Desktop.

- **Help menu**. This contains the Mac Help files, which contain information about all aspects of macOS High Sierra.

6 Navigating in High Sierra

macOS High Sierra uses

Multi-Touch Gestures for

navigating your apps and

documents. This chapter looks at

how to use these to get around.

Navigating with MacBooks

macOS High Sierra on the MacBook uses a number of physical gestures to navigate around the operating system, folders and files. This involves a much greater reliance on swiping on a trackpad or adapted mouse; techniques that have been imported from the iPhone and the iPad. These are known as Multi-Touch Gestures and work most effectively with the trackpad on MacBooks. Other devices can also be used to perform Multi-Touch Gestures:

- **A Magic Trackpad**. This is an external trackpad that works wirelessly via Bluetooth, but there should not really be any need for one with a MacBook.

- **A Magic Mouse**. This is an external mouse that works wirelessly via Bluetooth.

These devices, and the trackpad, work using a swiping technique with fingers moving over their surface. This should be done with a light touch; it is a gentle swipe, rather than any pressure being applied to the device.

The trackpads and Magic Mouse do not have any buttons in the same way as traditional devices. Instead, specific areas are clickable so that you can still perform left- and right-click operations:

Don't forget

The MacBook and MacBook Pro Retina display 13-inch both have Force Touch technology on the trackpad. This still allows for the usual range of Multi-Touch Gestures but can also be used for other functions, depending on the amount of pressure that is applied to the trackpad. Settings for this can be applied in the **Trackpad** section within **System Preferences**.

1 Click on the bottom-left corner for traditional left-click operations

2 Ctrl + click on the bottom-right corner for traditional right-click operations

Pointing and Clicking

A trackpad or Magic Mouse can be used to perform a variety of pointing and clicking tasks.

1 Tap with one finger in the middle of the trackpad or Magic Mouse to perform a single-click operation; e.g. to click on a button or click on an open window

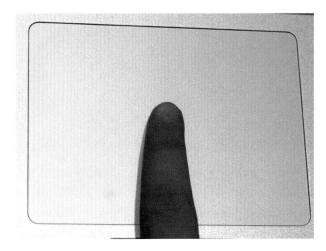

2 Tap with two fingers in the middle of the trackpad or Magic Mouse to access any contextual menus associated with an item (this is the equivalent of the traditional right-click with a mouse)

...cont'd

3 Highlight a word or phrase and double-tap with three fingers to see look-up information for the selected item. This is frequently a dictionary definition but it can also be a Wikipedia entry

Beware

If you have too many functions set using the same number of fingers, some of them may not work. See pages 114–116 for details about setting preferences for Multi-Touch Gestures.

104

4 Move over an item and drag with three fingers to move the item around the screen

macOS Scroll Bars

In macOS High Sierra, scroll bars in web pages and documents are more reactive to the navigational device being used on the computer. By default, with a trackpad or a Magic Mouse, scroll bars are only visible when scrolling is actually taking place. However, if a mouse is being used they will be visible permanently, although this can be changed for all devices. To perform scrolling with macOS High Sierra:

1 Scroll around a web page or document by swiping up or down on a trackpad or a Magic Mouse. As you move up or down, the scroll bar appears

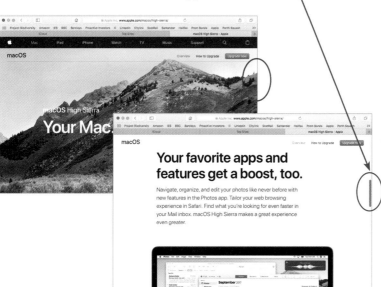

2 When you stop scrolling, the bar disappears to allow optimum viewing area for your web page or document

3 To change the scroll bar options, select **System Preferences** > **General** and select the required settings under **Show scroll bars:**

Show scroll bars: ● Automatically based on mouse or trackpad
○ When scrolling
○ Always

Scrolling and Zooming

One of the common operations on a computer is scrolling on a page, whether it is a web page or a document. Traditionally, this has been done with a mouse and a cursor. However, using a trackpad or Magic Mouse you can now do all of your scrolling with your fingers. There are a number of options for doing this:

Scrolling up and down

To move up and down web pages or documents, use two fingers on the trackpad and swipe up or down. The page moves in the opposite direction to the one in which you are swiping; i.e. if you swipe up, the page moves down, and vice versa:

Don't worry if you cannot immediately get the hang of Multi-Touch Gestures. It takes a bit of practice to get the correct touch and pressure on the trackpad or Magic Mouse.

1 Open a web page

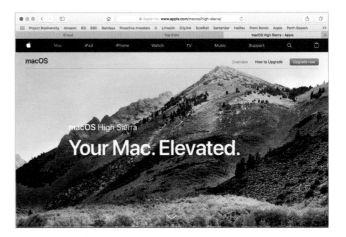

2 Position two fingers in the middle of the trackpad

3 Swipe them up to move down the page

Don't forget

When scrolling up and down pages, the gesture moves the page the opposite way; i.e. swipe down to move up the page, and vice versa.

4 Swipe them down to move up a page

...cont'd

Zooming in and out

To zoom in or out on web pages or documents:

1 To zoom in, position your thumb and forefinger in the middle of the trackpad

Don't forget

Pages can also be zoomed in on by double-tapping with two fingers.

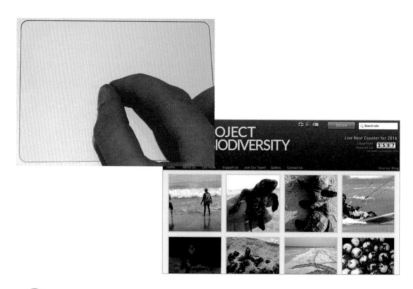

2 Spread them outwards to zoom in on a web page or document

3 To zoom out, position your thumb and forefinger at opposite corners of the trackpad

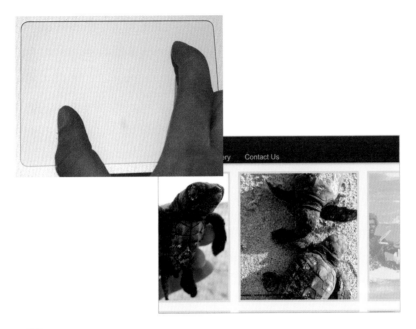

There is a limit to how far you can zoom in or out on a web page or document, to ensure that it does not distort the content too much.

4 Swipe them into the center of the trackpad to zoom out

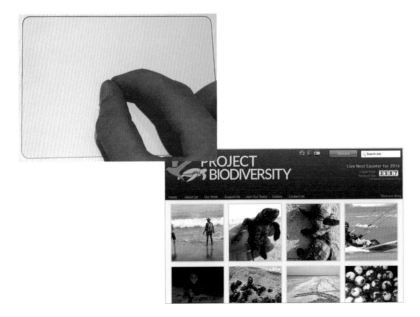

...cont'd

Moving between pages

With Multi-Touch Gestures it is possible to swipe between pages within a document. To do this:

1 Position two fingers to the left or right of the trackpad

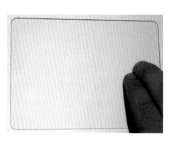

2 Swipe to the opposite side of the trackpad to move through the document

See pages 120-121 for details about using full-screen apps.

Moving between full-screen apps

In addition to moving between pages by swiping, it is also possible to move between different apps when they are in full-screen mode. To do this:

1 Position three fingers to the left or right of the trackpad

2 Swipe to the opposite side of the trackpad to move through the available full-screen apps

Showing the Desktop

To show the whole Desktop, regardless of how many files or apps are open:

1 Position your thumb and three fingers in the middle of the trackpad

2 Swipe to the opposite corners of the trackpad to display the Desktop

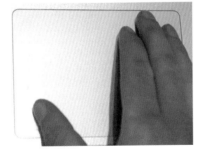

3 The Desktop is displayed, with all items minimized around the side of the screen

Mission Control and Spaces

Mission Control is a function in macOS High Sierra that helps you organize your open apps, full-screen apps and documents. It also enables you to quickly view the Desktop. Within Mission Control there are also Spaces, where you can group together similar types of documents. To use Mission Control:

Don't forget

Click on a window in Mission Control to access it and exit the Mission Control window.

1 Click on this button on the Dock, or

2 Swipe upwards with three fingers on the trackpad or Magic Mouse (or press Fn + F9 on the keyboard)

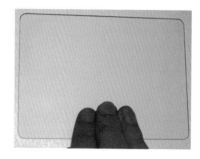

3 All open files and apps are visible via Mission Control

Beware

Any apps or files that have been minimized or closed do not appear within the main Mission Control window. Instead, they are located to the right of the dividing line on the Dock.

4 Move the cursor over the top of the Mission Control window to view the different Spaces and any apps in full-screen mode

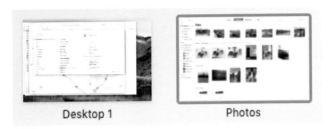

Desktop 1   Photos

Don't forget

Preferences for Spaces can be set within the Mission Control System Preference.

Spaces

The top level of Mission Control contains Spaces, which are areas into which you can group certain apps; e.g. the iWork apps such as Pages and Numbers. This means that you can access these apps independently from every other open item. This helps organize your apps and files. To use Spaces:

Hot tip

Create different Spaces for different types of content; e.g. one for productivity and one for entertainment.

113

1 Move the cursor over the top right-hand corner of Mission Control and click on the **+** symbol

2 A new **Space** is created along the top row of Mission Control

Desktop 2

Don't forget

When you create a new Space it can subsequently be deleted by moving the cursor over it and clicking on the cross at the left-hand corner. Any items that have been added to this Space are returned to the default Desktop Space.

3 Drag apps onto the Space. This can be accessed by clicking on the Space within Mission Control, and all of the apps that have been placed here will be available

Desktop 2

Multi-Touch Preferences

Some Multi-Touch Gestures only have a single action, which cannot be changed. However, others have options for changing the action for a specific gesture. This is done within the Trackpad preferences, where a full list of Multi-Touch Gestures is shown:

Point & Click preferences

1 Access the System Preferences and click on the **Trackpad** button

2 Click on the **Point & Click** tab

3 The actions are described on the left, with a graphical explanation on the right

Hot tip

When setting Multi-Touch Preferences try to avoid having too many gestures using the same number of fingers, in case some of them override the others.

114

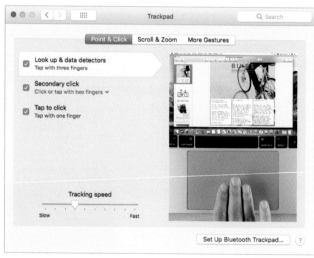

4 If there is a down arrow next to an option, click on it to change the way an action is activated

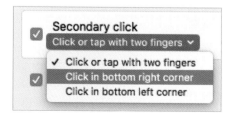

...cont'd

Scroll & Zoom preferences

1 Click on the **Scroll & Zoom** tab   `Scroll & Zoom`

2 The actions are described on the left, with a graphical explanation on the right

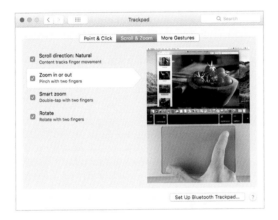

More Gestures preferences

1 Click on the **More Gestures** tab   `More Gestures`

2 The actions are described on the left, with a graphical explanation on the right

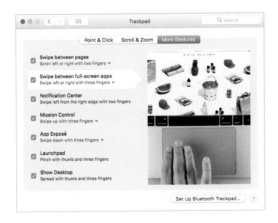

...cont'd

Multi-Touch Gestures

The full list of Multi-Touch Gestures, with their default actions are:

Point & Click

- Tap to click – tap with one finger.

- Secondary click – click or tap with two fingers.

- Look up – double-tap with three fingers.

- Three-finger drag – move with three fingers.

Scroll & Zoom

- Scroll direction: natural – content tracks finger movement.

- Zoom in or out – spread or pinch with two fingers.

- Smart zoom – double-tap with two fingers.

- Rotate – rotate with two fingers.

More Gestures

- Swipe between pages – scroll left or right with two fingers.

- Swipe between full-screen apps – swipe left or right with three fingers.

- Access Mission Control – swipe up with three fingers.

- Access the Notification Center – swipe left from the right-hand edge of the trackpad or Magic Trackpad.

- App Exposé – swipe down with three fingers. This displays the open windows for a specific app.

- Access Launchpad – pinch with thumb and three fingers.

- Show Desktop – spread with thumb and three fingers.

7 Working with Apps

Apps, or applications, are the programs with which you start putting High Sierra to use. This chapter looks at accessing your apps, and some of the functionality when using them. It also covers some of the most commonly-used apps, and looks at finding and downloading new ones from the online Apple App Store.

Launchpad

Even though the Dock can be used to store shortcuts to your applications, it is limited in terms of space. The full set of applications on your MacBook can be found in the Finder (in the Applications folder), but macOS High Sierra has a feature that allows you to quickly access and manage all of your applications. These include the ones that are pre-installed on your MacBook, and also any that you install yourself or download from the Apple App Store. This feature is called Launchpad. To use it:

If the apps take up more than one screen, swipe from right to left with two fingers to view the additional pages, or click on the dots at the bottom of the window.

1 Click once on this button on the Dock

2 All of the apps (applications) are displayed

Don't forget

To launch an app from within Launchpad, click on it once.

3 Similar types of apps can be grouped together in individual folders. By default, the Utilities are grouped in this way

4 To create a group of similar apps, drag the icon for one over another

5 The apps are grouped together in a folder and Launchpad gives it a name, based on the types of apps within the folder

To change the name, click on it once and overtype it with the new name

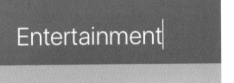

Don't forget

Some system apps (i.e. the ones that come pre-installed on your MacBook) cannot be removed from the Launchpad.

7 The folder appears within the **Launchpad** window

To remove an app, click and hold on it until it starts to jiggle and a cross appears. Click on the cross to remove it

Full-Screen Apps

When working with apps we all like to be able to see as much of a window as possible. With macOS High Sierra this is possible with the full-screen option. This allows you to expand an app with this functionality so that it takes up the whole of your monitor or screen with a minimum of toolbars visible. Some apps have this functionality, but some do not. To use full-screen apps:

1 By default, an app appears on the Desktop with other windows behind it

If the button in Step 2 is not visible then the app does not have the full-screen functionality.

2 Click on this button at the top left-hand corner of the app's window

3 The app is expanded to take up the whole window. The main Apple Menu bar and the Dock are hidden

4 To view the main Menu bar, move the cursor over the top of the screen

5 You can move between all full-screen apps by swiping with three fingers left or right on the trackpad

For more information about navigating with Multi-Touch Gestures see pages 102-116.

6 Move the cursor over the top left-hand corner of the screen and click on this button to close the full-screen functionality

7 In Mission Control, all of the open full-screen apps are shown in the top row

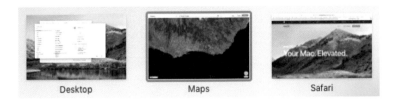

Desktop   Maps   Safari

High Sierra Apps

The built-in macOS High Sierra apps can be accessed from the Launchpad, as shown on page 118, or from the Applications folder within the Finder.

Some of the built-in macOS High Sierra apps include:

- **App Store**. This can be used to access the online App Store for viewing the range of apps there, and downloading new ones as required.

- **Calendar**. This can be used to record events and set reminders as required.

- **Contacts**. This is the macOS High Sierra address book, and contacts can be added with a range of details, including address, phone and mobile/cell number, email address and website address (if applicable).

- **FaceTime**. This can be used for video calls or voice calls to family and friends using a Mac or a mobile Apple device such as an iPhone or an iPad.

- **GarageBand**. This can be used to create digital music, by selecting an instrument and then recording the tune using a virtual keyboard.

- **iBooks**. This can be used to access the online iBooks Store and download ebooks that you want to read. Downloaded books are stored in the app.

- **iMovie**. This can be used to edit digital video that has been captured with a digital video camera or a smartphone.

- **iTunes**. This can be used to download music from the iTunes Store and then play tracks and albums. See page 127 for details.

- **Keynote**. This is Apple's presentation app that can be used to create slides in a linked presentation. It is part of the iWork suite of productivity apps.

- **Mail**. This is the macOS High Sierra default email app for sending and receiving emails. Photos and videos can be attached to emails with the app.

Don't forget

The iWork suite of apps (Keynote, Numbers and Pages) are available for qualifying MacBooks bought in or after October 2013. The apps can be downloaded, for free, from the App Store.

- **Maps**. This can be used to look up locations worldwide and also find directions between two different locations.

- **Messages**. This can be used to send text messages, including adding photos, videos and emojis. See page 125 for more details.

- **Notes**. This is Apple's note-taking app, which can be used to add checkboxes and hand-drawn notes. See pages 128-129 for details.

- **Numbers**. This is Apple's spreadsheet app that can be used to create spreadsheets for numerical calculations. It is part of the iWork suite.

- **Pages**. This is Apple's word processing app that can be used to create a range of documents, using templates if required. It is part of the iWork suite.

- **Photo Booth**. This is an app for creating funny and quirky photo effects.

- **Photos**. This is the replacement app for iPhoto and can be used to arrange, share and edit photos. See page 126 for details.

- **Preview**. This can be used to view files in a range of file formats such as JPEGs and GIFs for images, and also PDF files.

- **Reminders**. This can be used to set reminders on your MacBook. At the required time you will be alerted to the reminder.

- **Safari**. This is the macOS-specific web browser that supports tabbed browsing. See page 124 for details.

- **Siri**. This is Apple's digital voice assistant that is now available for macOS High Sierra. See pages 44-47 for details.

- **Time Machine**. This is the macOS's backup facility. See pages 174-177 for details.

Apps such as Notes and Reminders can be shared via the online iCloud facility. Ensure they are checked **On** within the iCloud System Preference. They can also be set to appear in the Notification Center via the Notifications System Preference.

123

Safari App

Safari is a web browser that is designed specifically to be used with macOS. It is similar in most respects to other browsers, and works seamlessly with High Sierra.

1 All of the controls are at the top of the browser

Toolbar   Address/Search bar (Smart Search)   Tabs

Bookmarks Bar and buttons

2 Click on this button to open a new tab. This will open in the Top Sites window, from where a new website can be opened, or the Smart Search box can be used

3 Click on this button to view all of the currently-open tabs, as thumbnails

4 Click on this button to **Share** a web page, via email, messages or social media

5 Click on this button to view the Safari **Sidebar**, containing bookmarks, Reading List and shared links to subscribed feeds

6 Click on this button to view the **Top Sites** window, displayed as thumbnails. Move the cursor over a thumbnail to access its controls for deleting it or pinning it to the Top Sites window

Messages App

The Messages app can be used to send and receive text messages over Wi-Fi from a MacBook with other macOS users, and also those using iOS on a mobile Apple device such as an iPhone or an iPad. These are known as iMessages. To use Messages:

1 Click on this button to start a new conversation

2 Click on this button and select a contact (these will be from your Contacts app). To send an iMessage, the recipient must have an Apple ID

The person, or people, with whom you are having a conversation is displayed in the left-hand panel

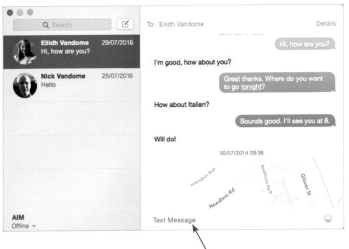

Hot tip

Photos and videos can also be added to iMessages, by dragging them from their location in the Finder into the text box.

The conversation continues down the right-hand panel. Click here to write a message and press **Return** to send

5 Click on this icon at the right-hand side of the text box to add large emojis to a message

Photos App

The Photos app can be used to view photos according to Years, Collections, Moments, Memories or at full size. This enables you to view your photos according to dates and times at which they were taken. They can also be edited and shared in the Photos app:

1 Click on these buttons at the top of the Photos window to move between **Years**, **Collections** and **Moments**

2 Double-click on a thumbnail to view it at full size

3 In full-size mode, click on the **Edit** button to access the editing options

Edit

4 Click on the **Memories** button in the left-hand sidebar to view collections of photos that are created by the app

Memories

iTunes App

The iTunes app can be used to play music and also access the iTunes Store for downloading music:

1 Open the iTunes app and click on this button to access the iTunes Store

Store

The iTunes Store contains thousands of songs and albums, from a variety of genres, that can be bought and downloaded to your MacBook

Click on the **Library** button to view the items that have been downloaded into your own music library on your MacBook. Double-click on an item to play it. Use the music controls to rewind, play/pause or fast-forward a track

Library

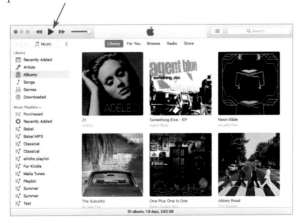

Hot tip

iTunes can also be used to play music CDs, by inserting the CD in an external (or internal) SuperDrive. In the iTunes window, click on the **Import CD** button if you want to import it into your iTunes library.

Import CD

Don't forget

Click on the **For You** button to access a window for subscribing to Apple Music. This gives access to the whole iTunes library of music, which can be streamed to your MacBook. There is a free three-month trial before the subscription starts.

For You

Notes App

It is always useful to have a quick way of making notes of everyday things, such as shopping lists, recipes or packing lists for traveling. With macOS High Sierra, the Notes app is perfect for this task. To use it:

Don't forget

Enable iCloud for Notes so that all of your notes will be backed up, and also available on all of your iCloud-enabled devices. You will also be able to access them by signing in to your account with your Apple ID at **www.icloud.com**

Don't forget

The first line of a note becomes its heading in the notes panel.

1 Click on this icon on the Dock, or in the Launchpad

2 The right-hand panel is where the note is created. The middle panel displays a list of all notes

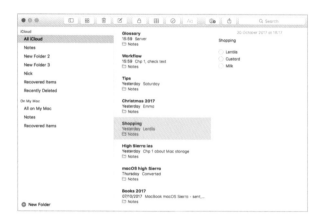

3 Click on this button to show or hide the left-hand panel in the Notes app, which displays the notes folders

4 Click on this button to add a new note

5 As more notes are added, the most recent appears at the top of the list in the middle panel. Double-click the new note to add text and edit formatting options (see next page)

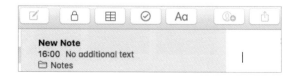

Cmd + click on a note heading and click on **Pin Note** to pin it to its position in the notes list. This is a new feature in macOS High Sierra.

Formatting notes

In macOS High Sierra there are a number of formatting options for the Notes app:

1 Enter a line of text and click on this button to add a check button

2 Click on the check button to add a tick, to indicate that an item has been completed

Highlight a piece of text and click on this button to access formatting options for it

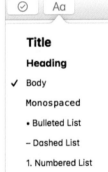

Click on this button on the Notes toolbar to add photos and videos, sketches, maps, websites, sound clips and documents to a note. Navigate to the required item and drag it into the note from the Attachments Browser

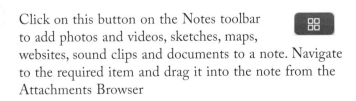

Click on this button to add a table to a note. This is a new feature in macOS High Sierra.

Don't forget

Click on the **Share** button to share a note with other people, via a range of other apps.

Click on this button to invite other people to have access to the note so they can view it and edit it.

Hot tip

Content can be added to notes from a range of other apps, such as Safari or the Photos app, by clicking on the **Share** button in the relevant app and selecting **Notes** as the option.

129

App Notifications

Notifications can be set up on the MacBook so that you can view a range of daily information and also see alerts from specified apps, such as Mail. To do this:

Hot tip

If you do not want notifications to appear for an item in the left-hand panel in Step 2, select **None** for the alert style and check **Off** the **Show in Notification Center** checkbox.

Hot tip

To change the items that appear in the Today panel, scroll down to the bottom of the panel and click on the **Edit** button. In the Edit window, items can be removed by clicking on the red circle next to them. New items can be added by clicking on the green circle next to them. Click on the **Done** button to finish editing the items.

1 Open System Preferences and click on the **Notifications** button

2 Click on an item in the left-hand panel to select it and click here to select the type of alert that appears for the notification. These appear on the MacBook Desktop screen

3 Click on this button in the top right-hand corner of the screen to view the Notification Center

4 Click on the **Today** tab to view items such as Calendar events for the current day, the weather forecast, Reminders and stock prices

5 Click on the **Notifications** tab to view notifications from the apps selected in Step 2

Accessing the App Store

The Apple App Store is an online facility where you can download and buy new apps. These cover a range of categories such as productivity, business and entertainment. When you select or buy an app from the App Store, it is downloaded automatically by Launchpad and appears here next to the rest of the apps.

To buy apps from the App Store you need to have an Apple ID. If you have not already set this up, it can be done when you first access the App Store. To use the App Store:

1 Click on this icon on the Dock or within the Launchpad

2 The Homepage of the App Store contains the current top featured apps

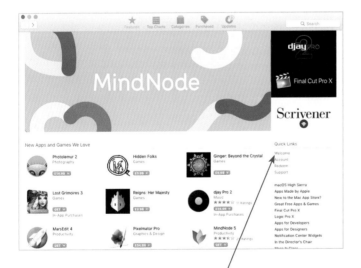

3 Your account information and **Quick Links** categories are listed at the right-hand side of the page

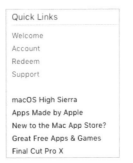

131

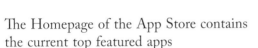

The App Store is an online function so you will need an internet connection to access it.

You can set up an Apple ID when you first set up your MacBook, or you can do it when you register for the App Store or the iTunes Store.

Downloading Apps

The App Store contains a wide range of apps: from small, fun apps to powerful productivity ones. However, downloading them from the App Store is the same regardless of the type of app. The only differences are whether they need to be paid for or not and the length of time they take to download. To download an app from the App Store:

Hot tip

When downloading apps, start with a free one first so that you can get used to the process before you download paid-for apps.

1 Browse through the App Store until you find the required app

Mimeo Photos
Photography

2 Click on the app to view a detailed description about it

3 Click on the button underneath the app icon to download it. If there is no charge for the app the button will say **Get**

If there is a charge for the app, the button will say **Buy App**

Enter your Apple ID account details and click on the **Buy** button to download the app

The progress of the download is displayed in a progress bar underneath the Launchpad icon on the Dock

Once it has been downloaded, the app is available within Launchpad

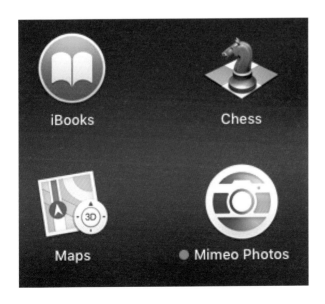

Don't forget

Depending on their size, different apps take differing amounts of time to be downloaded.

Don't forget

As you download more apps, additional pages will be created within the Launchpad to accommodate them.

Finding Apps

There are thousands of apps in the App Store and sometimes the hardest task is locating the ones you want. However, there are a number of ways in which finding apps is made as easy as possible.

1 Click on the **Featured** button

2 The main window has a range of categories such as New, Apps and Games We Love, and Our Favorite Mac Apps. At the right-hand side there is a panel with the current top **Paid** apps

Another way to find apps is to type a keyword into the Search box at the top right-hand corner of the App Store window.

134

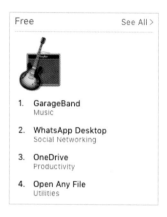

3 Underneath this is a list of the current top **Free** apps

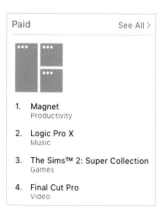

4 Click on the **Top Charts** button

5 The top apps for different categories are displayed

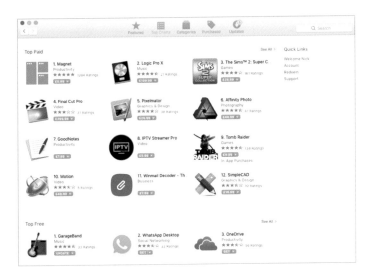

6 Click on the **Categories** button

7 Browse through the apps by specific categories, such as Business, Entertainment, and Finance

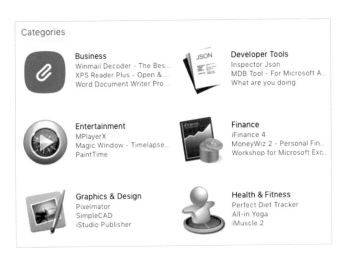

Managing Your Apps

Once you have bought apps from the App Store you can view details of ones you have purchased, and also install updated versions of them.

Purchased apps

To view your purchased apps:

1 Click on the **Purchased** button

2 Details of your purchased apps are displayed (including those that are free)

3 If a download of an app has been interrupted, click on the **Resume** button to continue with it

Updating apps

Improvements and fixes are being developed constantly, and these can be downloaded to ensure that all of your apps are up-to-date.

1 When updates are available this is indicated by a red, numbered circle on the **App Store** icon in the Dock

2 Click on the **Updates** button. Click on the **Update** button next to an app to update it, or the **Update All** button to update all of the applicable apps

8 Sharing High Sierra

This chapter looks at how to set up different user accounts and how to keep children safe, using parental controls.

Adding Users

macOS enables multiple users to access individual accounts on the same computer. If there are multiple users (i.e. two or more for a single machine), each person can sign on individually and access their own files and folders. This means that each person can log in to their own settings and preferences. All user accounts can be password-protected, to ensure that each user's environment is secure. To set up multiple user accounts:

Don't forget

Every computer with multiple users has at least one main user, also known as an administrator. This means that they have greater control over the number of items that they can edit and alter. If there is only one user on a computer, they automatically take on the role of the administrator. Administrators have a particularly important role to play when computers are networked together. Each computer can potentially have several administrators.

Don't forget

Each user can select their own icon or photo of themselves.

1 Click on the **System Preferences** icon on the Dock

2 Click on the **Users & Groups** icon

Users & Groups

3 The information about the current account is displayed. This is your own account, and the information is based on details you provided when you first set up your MacBook

4 Click on this icon to enable new accounts to be added (the padlock needs to be open)

Click the lock to prevent further changes.

5 Click on the **+** button to add a new account

6 Enter the details for the new account holder

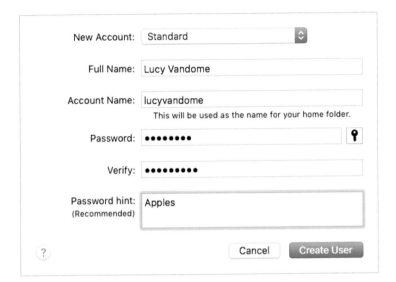

New Account:	Standard
Full Name:	Lucy Vandome
Account Name:	lucyvandome
	This will be used as the name for your home folder.
Password:	••••••••
Verify:	•••••••••
Password hint: (Recommended)	Apples

Cancel   Create User

7 Click on the **Create User** button

Create User

8 The new account is added to the list in the Users & Groups window, under **Other Users**

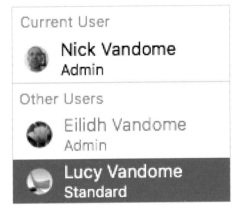

Current User

Nick Vandome
Admin

Other Users

Eilidh Vandome
Admin

Lucy Vandome
Standard

Don't forget

At Step 6, choose the type of account from the drop-down list. An **Administrator** account is one which allows the user to make system changes, and add or delete other users; a **Standard** account allows the user to use the functionality of the MacBook, but not change system settings; **Manage with Parental Controls** is an account that can have restrictions added to it; and **Sharing Only** is an account that allows guests to log in temporarily, without a password – when they log out, all files and information will be deleted from the guest account.

Don't forget

By default, you are the administrator of your own MacBook. This means that you can administer other user accounts.

139

Deleting Users

Once a user has been added, their name appears on the list in the Users & Groups dialog box. It is then possible to edit the details of a particular user or delete them altogether. To do this:

Always tell other users if you are planning to delete them from the system. Don't just remove them and then let them find out the next time they try to log in. If you delete a user, their personal files can be left untouched and can still be accessed (by selecting **Don't change the home folder** in Step 3).

1 Within **Users & Groups**, unlock the settings as shown on page 138, then select a user from the list

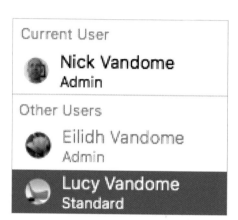

2 Click here to remove the selected person's user account

3 A warning box appears, to check if you really do want to delete the selected user. If you do, select the required option and click on the **Delete User** button

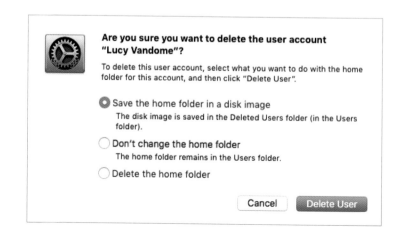

Fast User Switching

If there are multiple users on your macOS system, it is useful to be able to switch between them as quickly as possible. When this is done, the first user's session is retained so that they can return to it if required. To switch between users:

① In the Users & Groups window, click on the **Login Options** button

Unlock the settings before you start (see Step 4 on page 138).

② Check **On** the **Show fast user switching menu as** box, then close the window

☑ Show fast user switching menu as   Full Name ⌄

③ At the top-right of the screen, click on the current user's name

Nick Vandome

④ Click on the name of another user

When you switch between users, the first user remains logged in and their current session is retained intact.

141

⑤ Enter the relevant password (if required)

⑥ Click on this button to log in

Users can sign in from the Lock screen with a password by clicking on their own icon/name on the screen and entering the relevant details. If fast user switching is not used, each user has to log out before the next one can sign in.

Parental Controls

If children are using the MacBook, parents may want to restrict access to certain types of information that can be viewed, using Parental Controls. To do this:

Don't forget

Once Parental Controls are enabled, the account title for the user changes from **Standard** to **Managed**.

Hot tip

Parental Controls can also be accessed from the **Parental Controls** option in System Preferences.

1 Access **Users & Groups** and click on a username and check **On** the **Enable parental controls** box, then click on the **Open Parental Controls...** button

☑ Enable parental controls   Open Parental Controls...

2 Click on the **Apps** tab

Apps

3 Check **On** or **Off** the boxes for using the camera, multiplayer games and email contacts, as required

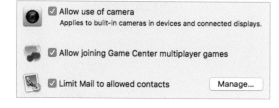
☑ Allow use of camera
Applies to built-in cameras in devices and connected displays.

☑ Allow joining Game Center multiplayer games

☑ Limit Mail to allowed contacts   Manage...

4 Check **On** this box if you want to limit the types of app that a user can access

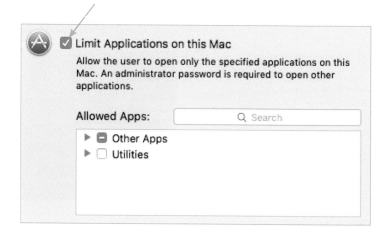
☑ Limit Applications on this Mac
Allow the user to open only the specified applications on this Mac. An administrator password is required to open other applications.

Allowed Apps: Q Search

▶ ☐ Other Apps
▶ ☐ Utilities

...cont'd

Web controls

1 Click on the **Web** tab

2 Check **On** this button to try to prevent access to websites with adult content

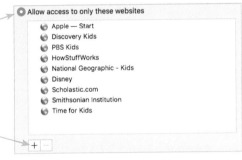

3 Alternatively, check **On** this button to specify websites that are suitable to be viewed. Click here to add more suitable websites

Stores controls

Hot tip

If you are setting web controls for a child, or grandchild, discuss this with them so they understand what you are doing and why. This could also be a good time to discuss some the issues of online security, such as never replying to any type of message or contact from people that you do not know.

1 Click on the **Stores** tab

2 Click here to disable or enable use of the iTunes and iBooks Stores

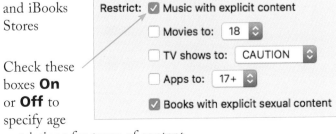

3 Check these boxes **On** or **Off** to specify age restrictions for types of content

...cont'd

Time controls

1 Click on the **Time** tab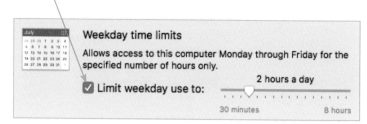

2 Check **On** this box to limit the amount of time the user can use the MacBook during weekdays

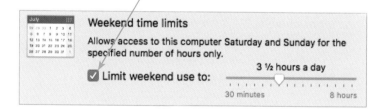

3 Check **On** this box to limit the amount of time the user can use the MacBook during weekends

4 Check **On** these boxes to determine the times at which the user cannot access their account

Privacy controls

1 Click on the **Privacy** tab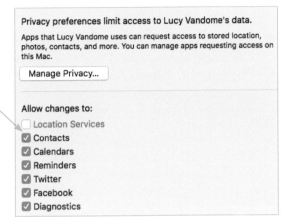

2 Check these boxes **On** or **Off** to enable the user to make changes to these apps, or not

Privacy preferences limit access to Lucy Vandome's data.

Apps that Lucy Vandome uses can request access to stored location, photos, contacts, and more. You can manage apps requesting access on this Mac.

Manage Privacy...

Allow changes to:

☐ Location Services
☑ Contacts
☑ Calendars
☑ Reminders
☑ Twitter
☑ Facebook
☑ Diagnostics

Other controls

1 Click on the **Other** tab

2 Check these items **On** or **Off** to turn off Siri, disable printers and scanners, block CD and DVD burning, restrict explicit language

☑ Turn off Siri & Dictation
Prevents the user from enabling Dictation in the Keyboard preferences and Siri in the Siri preference pane.

☐ Disable editing of printers and scanners
Prevents the user from changing printer settings, adding printers, and removing printers.

☐ Block CD and DVD burning in the Finder
Prevents the user from burning CDs and DVDs in the Finder.

☑ Restrict explicit language in Dictionary
Limits access to inappropriate content in sources such as dictionaries, thesauruses, and Wikipedia.

☐ Prevent the Dock from being modified
Prevents the user from modifying the contents of the Dock.

☑ Use Simple Finder
Provides a simplified view of the computer desktop for young or inexperienced users.

in the Dictionary, prevent the Dock being modified, and use a simplified version of the Finder for young or inexperienced users

High Sierra for Windows

General sharing

One of the historical complaints about Macs is that it is difficult to share files between them and Microsoft Windows computers. While this may have been true with some file types in years gone by, this is an issue that is becoming less and less important, particularly with High Sierra. Some of the reasons for this are:

- A number of popular file formats, such as PDFs (Portable Document Format) for documents and JPEGs (Joint Photographic Experts Group) for photos and images, are designed so that they can be used on both Mac and Windows platforms.

- A lot of software apps on the Mac have options for saving files into different formats, including ones that are specifically for Windows machines.

- Other popular apps, such as Microsoft Office, now have Mac versions and the resulting files can be shared on both formats.

Sharing with Boot Camp

For people who find it hard to live without Microsoft Windows, help is at hand even on a Mac. Macs have an app called Boot Camp that can be used to run a version of Windows on a Mac. This is only available with macOS. Once it has been accessed, a copy of Windows can then be installed and run. This means that if you have a non-Mac app that you want to use on your Mac, you can do so with Boot Camp.

Boot Camp is set up with the Boot Camp Assistant, which is located within the Utilities folder within the Applications folder (or from the Launchpad). Once this is run, you can then install either Windows XP, Vista, Windows 7, Windows 8 or Windows 10, which should run at its native speed.

Many file formats can be opened on both Macs and Windows PCs. Even Word, Excel and PowerPoint files can be exchanged, as long as each user has the relevant version of Office.

Boot Camp Assistant

9 MacBook Networking

This chapter looks at how to use your MacBook to create and work with networks, for sharing information.

Connecting to the internet is also another form of network connection.

If you have two Macs to be networked and they are in close proximity, then this can be achieved with an Ethernet crossover cable. If you have more than two computers, then this is where an Ethernet hub is required. In either case, there is no need to connect to the internet to achieve the network.

Networking Overview

Before you start sharing files directly between computers, you have to connect them together. This is known as networking and can be done with two computers in the same room, or with thousands of computers in a major corporation. If you are setting up your own small network it will be known in the computing world as a Local Area Network (LAN). When setting up a network, there are various pieces of hardware that are initially required to join all of the required items together. Once this has been done, software settings can be applied for the networked items. Some of the items of hardware that may be required include:

- **A network card**. This is known as a Network Interface Card (NIC), and all recent Macs have them built in.

- **A wireless router**. This is for a wireless network, which is increasingly the most common way to create a network, via Wi-Fi. The router is connected to a telephone line, and the computer then communicates with it wirelessly.

- **An Ethernet port and Ethernet cable**. This enables you to make the physical connection between devices. Ethernet cables come in a variety of forms, but the one you should be looking for is the Cat7 type, as this allows for the fastest transfer of data. If you are creating a wireless network then you will not require these.

- **A hub**. This is a piece of hardware with multiple Ethernet ports that enables you to connect all of your devices together and lets them communicate with each other. However, conflicts can occur with hubs if two devices try to send data through one at the same time.

- **A switch**. This is similar in operation to a hub but it is more sophisticated in its method of data transfer, thus allowing all of the machines on the network to communicate simultaneously, unlike a hub.

Once you have worked out all of the devices that you want to include on your network, you can arrange them accordingly. Try to keep the switches and hub within relative proximity of a power supply and, if you are using cables, make sure they are laid out safely.

Ethernet network

The cheapest and easiest way to network computers is to create an Ethernet network. This involves buying an Ethernet hub or switch, which enables you to connect several devices to a central point; i.e. the hub or switch. All Apple computers and most modern printers have an Ethernet connection, so it is possible to connect various devices, not just computers. Once all of the devices have been connected by Ethernet cables, you can then start applying network settings.

AirPort network

Another option for creating a network is using Apple's own wireless system, AirPort. This creates a wireless network, and there are two main options used by Apple computers: AirPort Express, using the IEEE 802.11n standard, which is more commonly known as Wi-Fi; and the newer AirPort Extreme, using the next-generation IEEE 802.11ac standard, which is up to five times faster than the 802.11n standard. Thankfully, AirPort Express and Extreme are also compatible with devices based on the older IEEE standards, 802.11b/g/n, so one machine loaded with AirPort Extreme can still communicate wirelessly with the older AirPort version.

One of the main issues with a wireless network is security, since it is possible for someone with a wireless-enabled machine to access your wireless network if they are within range. However, in the majority of cases the chances of this happening are fairly slim, although it is an issue about which you should be aware.

The basic components of a wireless network between Macs is an AirPort card (either AirPort Express or AirPort Extreme) installed in all of the required machines, and an AirPort base station that can be located anywhere within 150 meters of the AirPort-enabled computers. Once the hardware is in place, wireless-enabled devices can be configured by using the AirPort Setup Assistant utility found in the Utilities folder. After AirPort has been set up, the wireless network can be connected. All of the wireless-enabled devices should then be able to communicate with each other, without the use of a multitude of cables.

Wireless network

A wireless network can also be created with a standard wireless router, rather than using the AirPort option.

Another method for connecting items wirelessly is called Bluetooth. This covers much shorter distances than AirPort, and is generally used for items like printers and cellphones. Bluetooth devices can be connected by using the Bluetooth Setup Assistant in the Utilities folder.

AirPort Time Capsule is a method of backing up, using Wi-Fi instead of a cable connection. It offers up to 3TB of storage and is designed to work with Time Machine (see pages 174-177).

Network Settings

Once you have connected the hardware required for a network, you can start applying the network settings that are required for connecting to the internet, for online access.

1 In **System Preferences**, click on the **Network** button

2 For a wireless connection, click on the **Turn Wi-Fi On** button

3 Details of wireless settings are displayed

4 If you are already connected to a network, this will be shown in the **Status** section. If you are connected to a wireless network, the connection will be via AirPort

> **Status: Connected**   Turn Wi-Fi Off
> Wi-Fi is connected to PlusnetWireless792287 and has the IP address 192.168.1.125.

5 The network name is shown here

> Network Name: PlusnetWireless792287

6 Check **On** this box if you want to be notified before joining a new network

> ☑ **Ask to join new networks**
> Known networks will be joined automatically. If no known networks are available, you will be asked before joining a new network.

7 For a cable connection, connect an Ethernet cable

8 Details of the cable settings are displayed

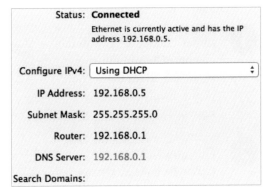

For an Ethernet connection you need to have an Ethernet cable connected to your MacBook and the router.

9 Click on the **Advanced...** button to access a range of options for both Wi-Fi and cable network connections

Advanced...

10 Click on the tabs at the top of the window to view the advanced options for each type of connection

Connecting to a Network

Connecting as a registered user

To connect as a registered user (usually as yourself when you want to access items on another one of your own computers):

Don't forget

Your username and password are specified in the **Accounts** section of System Preferences.

1 Other connected computers on the network will show up in the **Shared** section in the Finder. Click on a networked computer

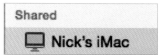
Shared
🖥 Nick's iMac

2 Click on the **Connect As...** button

Connect As...

3 Check **On** the **Registered User** button and enter your username and password

Enter your name and password for the server "Nick's iMac".

Connect as: ○ Guest
⦿ Registered User
○ Using an Apple ID

Name: nickvandome

Password: |

☐ Remember this password in my keychain

Cancel   Connect

Don't forget

You can disconnect from a networked computer by ejecting it in the Finder, in the same way as you would a removable drive, such as a DVD or flashdrive (see page 32).

4 Click on the **Connect** button

5 The public folders and home folder of the networked computer are available to the registered user. Double-click on an item to view its contents

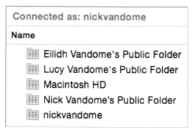

Connected as: nickvandome

Name

⬚ Eilidh Vandome's Public Folder
⬚ Lucy Vandome's Public Folder
⬚ Macintosh HD
⬚ Nick Vandome's Public Folder
⬚ nickvandome

...cont'd

Guest users

Guest users on a network are users other than yourself, or other registered users, to whom you want to limit access to your files and folders. Guests only have access to a folder called the Drop Box in your own Public folder. To share files with guest users, you have to first copy them into the Drop Box. To do this:

Drop Box is not the same as the Dropbox app. This is a cloud storage and backup facility.

1 Create a file and select **File** > **Save** from the Menu bar

2 Navigate to your own home folder (this is created automatically by macOS and is displayed in the Finder sidebar)

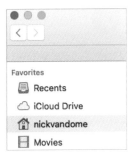

If another user is having problems accessing the files in your Drop Box, check the permissions settings assigned to the files (see page 186 for further details).

3 Double-click on the **Public** folder

4 Double-click on the **Drop Box** folder

The contents of the Drop Box can be accessed by other users on the same computer, as well as by users on a network.

5 Save the file into the Drop Box

153

...cont'd

Accessing a Drop Box
To access files in a Drop Box:

Don't forget

It is better to copy files into the Drop Box rather than moving them from their current location completely.

Hot tip

Set permissions for how the Drop Box operates by selecting it in the Finder and Ctrl + clicking on it. Select **Get Info** from the menu, and apply the required settings under the **Ownership & Permissions** heading.

1 Double-click on a networked computer in the Finder

2 Click on the **Connect As...** button in the Finder window

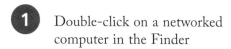

3 Select the **Guest** button

4 Click on the **Connect** button

Connect

5 Double-click on a user's public folder

6 Double-click on the Drop Box folder to access the files within it

File Sharing

One of the main reasons for creating a network of two or more computers is to share files between them. On networked MacBooks, this involves setting them up so that they can share files and then access them.

Setting up file sharing
To set up file sharing on a networked MacBook:

1 Click on the **System Preferences** icon on the Dock

2 Click on the **Sharing** icon and click on the padlock to unlock the settings, as shown on page 138

Sharing

Don't forget

If no file-sharing options are enabled in the Sharing preferences window, no other users will be able to access your computer or your files, even on a network.

3 Check **On** the boxes next to the items you want to share (the most common items to share are files and printers)

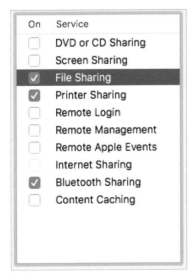

On	Service
☐	DVD or CD Sharing
☐	Screen Sharing
☑	File Sharing
☑	Printer Sharing
☐	Remote Login
☐	Remote Management
☐	Remote Apple Events
☐	Internet Sharing
☑	Bluetooth Sharing
☐	Content Caching

Hot tip

Networks can also be created, and items shared, between Macs and Windows-based PCs.

4 Click on the padlock to close it and prevent more changes

Sharing with AirDrop

Files can also be shared between Mac computers using the AirDrop feature. This enables the devices to connect wirelessly, and you can then share content between them. To do this:

1 In the Finder sidebar, click on the **AirDrop** button

2 Other users in range with AirDrop are shown in the main Finder window

3 Drag content from another Finder window (or the Desktop) over the other user's icon to share it with them

4 Content that has been shared from another device is initially placed in the **Downloads** folder in the Finder. It can then be copied from here and placed in another location, if required

10 MacBook Mobility

MacBooks are ideal for mobile working, for business or pleasure. This chapter looks at being mobile with your MacBook, including protecting it and security concerns.

Transporting Your MacBook

When you are going traveling, either for business or pleasure, your MacBook can be a very valuable companion. It can be used to download photographs from a digital camera, download movies from a digital video camera, keep a diary or business notes, and keep a record of your itinerary and important documents. Also, in many parts of the world it can access the internet via wireless hotspots so that you can view the web and send emails. However, when you are traveling with your MacBook it is sensible to transport this valuable asset in as safe and secure a way as possible. Some of the options include:

MacBook cases and sleeves

There is a range of MacBook cases and sleeves designed specifically for providing protection for the MacBook. They can be bought from the Apple website or Apple stores.

Metal case

If you are concerned that your MacBook may be in danger of physical damage when you are on the road, you may want to consider a more robust metal case. These are similar to those used by photographers and, depending on its size and design, you may also be able to include any photographic equipment.

Backpacks

A serious option for transporting your MacBook while you are traveling is a small backpack. This can either be a standard backpack or a backpack specifically designed for a MacBook. The latter is clearly a better option as the MacBook will fit more securely and there are also pockets designed for accessories.

Don't forget

A backpack for carrying a MacBook can be more comfortable than a shoulder bag, as it distributes the weight more evenly.

Keeping Your MacBook Safe

By most measures, MacBooks are valuable items. However, in a lot of countries around the world their relative value can be a lot more than it is to their owners: in some countries the value of a MacBook could easily equate to a month's, or even a year's, wages. Even in countries where their relative value is not so high they can still be seen as a lucrative opportunity for thieves. Therefore, it is important to try to keep your MacBook as safe as possible when you are traveling with it, either abroad or at home. Some points to consider in relation to this are:

- If possible, keep your MacBook with you at all times; i.e. transport it in a piece of luggage that you can carry rather than having to put it into a large case.

- Never hand over your MacBook, or any of your belongings, to any local who promises to look after them.

- If you do have to detach yourself from your MacBook, put it somewhere secure such as a hotel safe.

- When you are traveling, keep your MacBook as unobtrusive as possible. This is where a backpack carrying case can prove useful, as it is not immediately apparent that you are carrying a MacBook.

- Do not use your MacBook in areas where you think it may attract undue interest from the locals, particularly in obviously poor areas. For instance, if you are in a local cafe the appearance of a MacBook may create unwanted attention for you. If in doubt, wait until you get back to your hotel.

- If you are accosted by criminals who demand your MacBook, hand it over. No piece of equipment is worth suffering physical injury for.

- If you are abroad make sure your MacBook is covered by your travel insurance. If not, get separate insurance for it.

- Trust your instincts with your MacBook. If something doesn't feel right, don't do it.

Save your important documents onto a flashdrive, or an external hard drive, on a daily basis when you are traveling and keep this away from your MacBook. Alternatively, back up to iCloud when Wi-Fi is available. This way, you will still have these items if your MacBook is lost or stolen.

Temperature Extremes

Traveling consists of seeing a lot of different places and cultures, but it also invariably involves different extremes of temperature: a visit to the pyramids of Egypt can see the mercury in the upper reaches of the thermometer, while a trip to Alaska would encounter much colder conditions. Whether it is hot or cold, looking after your MacBook is an important consideration in extremes of temperature.

Beware

If a MacBook gets too hot it could buckle the casing, making it difficult to close.

Heat

When traveling in hot countries, the best way of avoiding any heat damage to your MacBook is to prevent it from getting too hot in the first place:

- Do not place your MacBook in direct sunlight.

- Keep your MacBook insulated from the heat.

- Do not leave your MacBook in an enclosed space, such as a car. Not only can this get very hot, but the sun's power can be increased by the vehicle's glass.

Hot tip

Wrap your MacBook in something white, such as a T-shirt or a towel, to insulate it against extreme heat.

Cold

Again, it is best to avoid your MacBook getting too cold in the first place, and this can be done by following similar precautions to those for heat. However, if your MacBook does suffer from extremes of cold, allow it to warm up to normal room temperature again before you try to use it. This may take a couple of hours, but it will be worth the wait, rather than risking damaging the delicate computing elements inside.

Dealing with Water

Water is one of the greatest enemies of any electrical device, and MacBooks are no different. This is of particular relevance to anyone who is traveling near water with their MacBook, such as on a boat or ship, or using their MacBook near a swimming pool or a beach. If you are near water with your MacBook then you must bear the following in mind:

- **Avoid water**. The best way to keep your MacBook dry is to keep it away from water whenever possible. For instance, if you want to update your notes or download some photographs, then it would be best to do this in an indoor environment, rather than sitting near water.

- **Keep dry**. If you think you will be transporting your MacBook near water then it is a good precaution to protect it with some form of waterproof bag. There is a range of "dry-bags" that are excellent for this type of occasion and they remain waterproof even if fully immersed in water. These can be bought from outdoor suppliers.

- **Dry out**. If the worst does occur and your MacBook does get a good soaking, all is not necessarily lost. However, you will have to ensure that it is fully dried out before you try to use it again. Never turn it on if it is still wet.

Power Sockets

Different countries and regions around the world use different types of power sockets, and this is an issue when you are traveling with your MacBook. Wherever you are going in the world, it is vital to have an adapter that will fit the sockets in the countries you intend to visit. Otherwise, you will not be able to charge your MacBook battery.

There are over a dozen different types of plugs and sockets used around the world, with the four most popular being:

North America, Japan
This is a two-point plug and socket.
The pins on the plug are flat and parallel.

Power adapters can be bought for all regions around the world. There are also kits that provide all of the adapters together. These provide connections for anywhere worldwide.

Continental Europe
This is a two-point plug and socket.
The pins are rounded.

Australasia, China, Argentina
This is a three-point socket that can accommodate either a two- or a three-pin plug. In a two-pin plug, the pins are angled in a V shape.

UK
This is a three-point plug and socket.
The pins are rectangular.

Airport Security

Because of the increased global security following terrorist attacks, including those on planes or at airports, levels of airport security have been greatly increased around the world. This has implications for all travelers, and if you are traveling with a MacBook, this will add to the security scrutiny you will face. When dealing with airport security when traveling with a MacBook, there are some issues you should always keep in mind:

- Keep your MacBook with you at all times. Unguarded baggage at airports immediately raises suspicion, and it can make life very easy for thieves.

- Carry your MacBook in a small bag so you can take it on board as hand luggage. On no account should it be put in with your luggage that goes in the hold.

- X-ray machines at airports will not harm your MacBook. However, if anyone tries to scan it with a metal detector, ask them if they can inspect it by hand instead.

- Keep a careful eye on your MacBook when it goes through the X-ray conveyor belt, and try to be there at the other side as soon as it emerges. There have been some stories of people causing a commotion at the security gate just after someone has placed their MacBook on the conveyor belt. While everyone's attention (including yours) is distracted, an accomplice takes the MacBook from the conveyor belt. If you are worried about this you can ask for the security guard to hand-check your MacBook rather than putting it on the conveyor belt.

- Make sure the battery of your MacBook is fully charged. This is because you may be asked to turn on your MacBook to verify that it is just that, and not some other device disguised as a MacBook. This check has become increasingly common in recent years due to security threats, and for some countries, such as the US, digital devices have to be turned on.

- When you are on the plane, keep the MacBook in the storage area under your seat, rather than in the overhead locker, so you know where it is at all times. Also, it could cause a serious injury if it fell out of an overhead locker.

Beware

If there is any kind of distraction when you are going through airport security it could be because someone is trying to divert your attention in order to steal your MacBook.

Hot tip

When traveling through airport security, leave your MacBook in Sleep mode, so it can be powered up quickly if anyone needs to check that it works properly.

Some Apps for Traveling

When you are traveling with your MacBook you can use it for productivity tasks with the iWork suite of Pages, Numbers and Keynote. In addition, Safari can be used to connect wirelessly to the web, and you can use iTunes for listening to music and Photos for your photos. There are also some other built-in apps that can be useful when you are traveling:

- **Notes**. Use this to create notes relating to your trip, ranging from Things to Pack lists to health information and travel details such as your itinerary. It is also a good option for keeping track of important items such as passport numbers.

- **iBooks**. Books are an ideal traveling companion, and with this app you do not have to worry about being weighed down by a lot of heavy volumes.

- **Maps**. This is the perfect app for researching cities abroad so that you can start to feel at home as soon as you arrive. You can view maps in standard or 3D satellite view, and also get directions between two locations.

Hot tip

For some locations, Maps has an automated 3D tour of a city. If this is available for the location being viewed, a **Flyover Tour** button will appear. Click on this to begin the flyover tour.

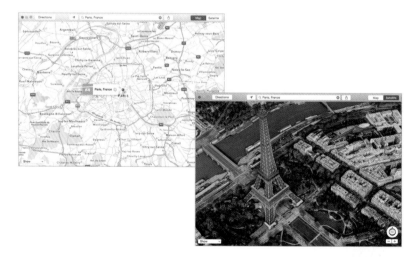

- **FaceTime**. You can use your MacBook to send emails and text messages when you are away from home, but FaceTime allows you to see people too, with voice and video calls.

11 Battery Issues

Battery power is crucial to a MacBook. This chapter shows how to get the best from your battery.

Power Consumption

Battery life for each charge of MacBook batteries is one area that engineers have worked very hard on since MacBooks were first introduced. For the latest models of MacBooks, the average battery life for each charge is approximately 10-11 hours. However, this is dependent on the power consumption of the MacBook; i.e. how much power is being used to perform particular tasks. Power-intensive tasks will reduce the battery life of each charge cycle. These types of tasks include:

- Watching a DVD.
- Editing digital photos or video.
- Browsing the web.
- Listening to music.

Click on the battery icon to show or hide the percentage figure next to it (see next page).

When you are using your MacBook you can always monitor how much battery power you currently have available. This is shown by the battery icon that appears at the top right on the Apple Menu bar. On battery power, the power level indicator is a solid color; on charge, it has a lightning symbol on it:

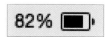 

As the battery runs down, the monitor bar turns red as a warning:

Because of the vital role the battery plays in relation to your MacBook, it is important to try to conserve its power as much as possible. To do this:

- Where possible, use the mains adapter rather than the battery when using your MacBook.
- Use the Sleep function when you are not actively using your MacBook (see page 52).
- Use power management functions to save battery power (see next page).

Power management

To access power management options, click on the battery icon on the Apple Menu bar. This shows the current battery source and the amount of power left, or the amount of charge in the battery. Click on the **Show Percentage** option to display

or hide the percentage figure for the amount of charge left in the battery. The Energy Saver preferences can be accessed here by clicking on the **Open Energy Saver Preferences...** link, or:

1 Access the **System Preferences** and click on the **Energy Saver** button

2 The **Energy Saver** window has a number of settings for the operation of your MacBook battery (see next two pages)

If you are undertaking an energy-intensive task, such as browsing the web, try to use the external AC/DC power cable rather than the battery, otherwise the battery may drain quite quickly, causing the MacBook to close down completely.

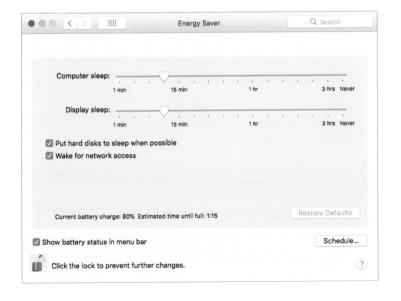

Energy Saver

MacBooks have options for how the battery is managed within the Energy Saver System Preference. These allow you to set things like individual power settings for the battery, and to view how much charge is left in the battery. To use the Energy Saver:

1 Access the **System Preferences** and click on the **Energy Saver** button

Energy
Saver

2 When the MacBook is on battery power, drag the sliders to specify when the computer and the display are put to sleep; i.e. in a state of hibernation

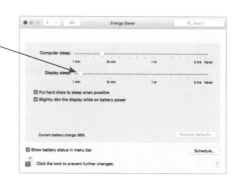

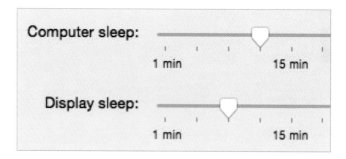

3 Check **On** these boxes to perform the required tasks

☑ Put hard disks to sleep when possible
☑ Slightly dim the display while on battery power

4 Check **On** this box to display the battery status at the top right-hand corner of the Apple Menu bar

☑ Show battery status in menu bar

5 Click on the **Schedule...** button   Schedule...

6 Select settings if you want your MacBook to wake up and sleep at pre-defined times

| ☑ Start up or wake | Every Day ⌄ | at | 09:00 ⌄ |
| ☑ Sleep ⌄ | Every Day ⌄ | at | 21:00 ⌄ |

Scheduled start up will only occur when a power adapter is connected to your Mac.

(?)   Cancel   OK

7 When the MacBook is connected with the power adapter, the options are similar. Drag the sliders to specify when the computer and the display are put to sleep (i.e. in a state of hibernation) in the same way as for when the MacBook is on battery power

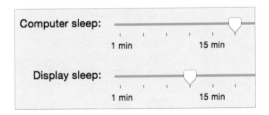

Computer sleep:
1 min   15 min

Display sleep:
1 min   15 min

Don't forget

With the power adapter it is acceptable to set longer periods before the computer or the display go to sleep.

8 Check **On** these boxes to perform the required tasks

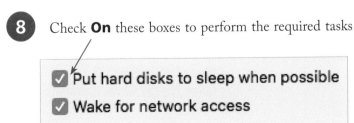

☑ Put hard disks to sleep when possible
☑ Wake for network access

Charging the Battery

MacBook batteries are charged using an AC/DC adapter, which can also be used to power the MacBook instead of the battery. If the MacBook is turned on and is being powered by the AC/DC adapter, the battery will be charged at the same time, although at a slower rate than if it is being charged when the MacBook is turned off.

The AC/DC adapter should be supplied with a new MacBook and consists of a cable and a power adapter. To charge a MacBook battery using an AC/DC adapter:

Don't forget

A MacBook battery can be charged whether the MacBook is turned on or off. It charges more quickly if the MacBook is not in use.

170

1 Connect the AC/DC adapter and the cable and plug it into the mains socket

2 Attach the AC/DC adapter to the MacBook and turn it on at the mains  socket. When it is attached, this battery icon is displayed on the Apple Menu bar, including the amount of charge in the battery, as a percentage

3 Click on the battery icon to view how long until the battery is charged, and the power source

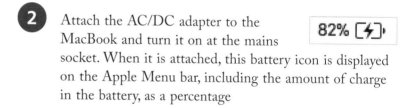

4 When using the battery, this is displayed as the power source

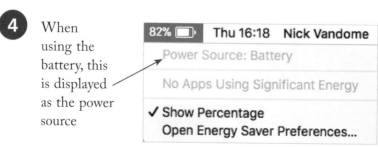

Dead and Spare Batteries

No energy source lasts forever, and MacBook batteries are no exception to this rule. Over time, the battery will operate less efficiently until it will not be possible to charge the battery at all. With average usage, most MacBook batteries should last approximately five years, although they will start to lose performance before this and become less efficient. Some signs of a dead MacBook battery are:

- Nothing happens when the MacBook is turned on using just battery power.

- The MacBook shuts down immediately if it is being run on the AC/DC adapter and the cord is suddenly removed.

- The following window appears a few minutes or immediately after you have charged the battery and then started to use your MacBook on battery power:

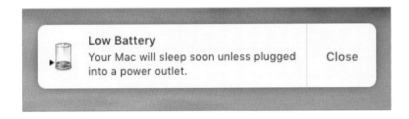

Low Battery
Your Mac will sleep soon unless plugged into a power outlet.   Close

Spare battery

Depending on how and where you use your MacBook, it might be worth considering buying a spare battery. Although these are not cheap, it can be a valuable investment, particularly if you spend a lot of time traveling with your MacBook and you are not always near a source of mains electricity. In situations like this, a spare battery could enable you to keep using your MacBook if your original battery runs out of power.

MacBook batteries can be bought from the Apple website or from an Apple store. However, they need to be fitted by an Apple store or a recognized Apple reseller.

When you are warned about a low battery, save all of your current work and either close down or switch to using an external AC/DC cable for powering your MacBook.

If you think that your battery may be losing its performance, make sure that you save your work at regular intervals. Although you should do this anyway, it is more important if there is a chance of your battery running out of power.

It is possible to replace a MacBook battery yourself but this is not advised as it would almost certainly invalidate the warranty.

Battery Troubleshooting

If you look after your MacBook battery well, it should provide you with several years of mobile computing power. However, there are some problems that may occur with the battery:

- It won't keep its charge even when connected to an AC/DC adapter. The battery is probably flat and should be replaced with a new one. (Even if the battery is flat, the MacBook will still operate using the AC/DC adapter.)

- It only charges up a limited amount. Over time, MacBook batteries become less efficient and so do not hold their charge so well. One way to try to improve this is to drain the battery completely before it is charged again.

- It keeps its charge but runs down quickly. This can be caused by using a lot of power-hungry applications on the MacBook. The more work the MacBook has to do to run applications, such as those involving videos or games, the more power will be required from the battery, and the faster it will run down.

- The MacBook only works when it is connected with the adapter. This is another sign that the battery is probably nearly flat and should be replaced.

- It is fully charged but does not appear to work. The battery may have become damaged in some way, such as from being in contact with water. If you know the battery is damaged in any way, take it to an Apple Store or a recognized Apple reseller and ask if the battery can be replaced. If the battery has been in contact with liquid, dry it out completely before trying to use it again. If it is thoroughly dry, it may work again.

- It gets very hot when in operation. This could be caused by a faulty battery, and it can be dangerous and lead to a fire. If in doubt, turn off the MacBook immediately and consult Apple. In some cases, faulty batteries can be recalled, so keep an eye on the Apple website to see if there are any details of this if you are concerned. Even in normal operation, MacBook batteries can feel quite warm. Get to know the normal temperature of your battery, so you can judge whether it is getting too hot or not.

Hot tip

If you are not going to be using your MacBook for an extended period of time, turn it off and store it in a safe, dry, cool place.

12 MacBook Maintenance

Despite its stability, macOS still benefits from a robust maintenance regime. This chapter looks at ways to keep macOS in top shape, ensure downloaded apps are as secure as possible, and some general troubleshooting.

Time Machine

Time Machine is a feature of macOS that gives you great peace of mind. In conjunction with an external hard drive, it creates a backup of your whole system, including folders, files, apps and even the macOS operating system itself.

Once it has been set up, Time Machine takes a backup every hour, and you can then go into Time Machine to restore any files that have been deleted or become corrupt.

Setting up Time Machine

To use Time Machine, it first has to be set up. This involves attaching a hard drive to your MacBook via cable or wirelessly, depending on the type of hard drive you have. To set up Time Machine:

Make sure that you have an external hard drive that is larger than the contents of your MacBook, otherwise Time Machine will not be able to back it all up.

174

An external hard drive must be connected in order to use Time Machine. Or, you could use AirPort Time Capsule, which is a method of backing up using Wi-Fi instead of a cable connection. It offers up to 3TB of storage and is designed to work with Time Machine.

1 Click on the **Time Machine** icon on the Dock, or access it in System Preferences

2 You will be prompted to set up Time Machine

3 Click on the **Set Up Time Machine** button

4 In the Time Machine System Preferences window, click on the **Select Disk...** button

5 Connect an external hard drive and select it from the **Available Disks** list

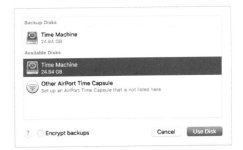

6 Click on the **Use Disk** button

7 In the Time Machine window, check **On** the **Back Up Automatically** button

8 The backup will begin. The initial backup copies your whole system and can take several hours. Subsequent hourly backups only look at items that have been changed since the previous backup

9 The record of backups and the schedule for the next one are shown here

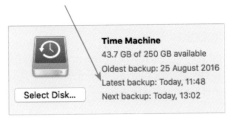

Beware

When you first set up Time Machine, it copies everything on your MacBook. Depending on the type of connection you have for your external drive, this could take several hours. Because of this, it is a good idea to have a hard drive with a USB 3.0 or Thunderbolt connection to make it as fast as possible.

Don't forget

If you stop the initial backup before it has been completed, Time Machine will remember where it has stopped and resume the backup from this point.

...cont'd

Using Time Machine

Once Time Machine has been set up, it can then be used to go back in time to view items in an earlier state. To do this:

1 Access an item on your MacBook and delete it. In this example, the folder **Apple Computing** has been deleted

2 Click on the **Time Machine** icon

3 Time Machine displays the selected window in its current state (the Apple Computing folder is deleted). Earlier versions are stacked behind it

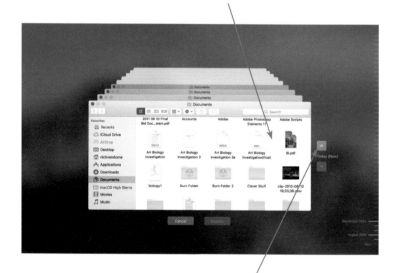

4 Click on the arrows to move through the open items, or select a time or date from the scale to the right of the arrows

5 Another way to move through the Time Machine is to click on the pages behind the first one. This brings the selected item to the front

6 Click on the **Restore** button to restore any items that have been deleted (in this case, the Apple Computing folder)

Restore

Don't forget

Items are restored from the Time Machine backup disk; i.e. the external hard drive.

7 Click on the **Cancel** button to return to your normal environment

Cancel

8 The deleted folder **Apple Computing** is now restored to its original location

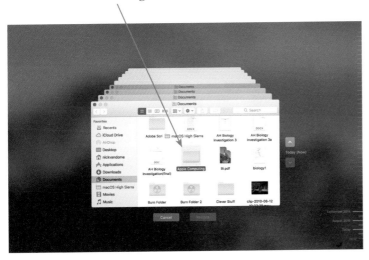

Disk Utility

Disk Utility is a utility app that allows you to perform certain testing and repair functions for macOS. It incorporates a variety of functions and is a good option for both general maintenance and if your computer is not running as it should.

Each of the functions within Disk Utility can be applied to specific drives and volumes. However, it is not possible to use the macOS startup disk within Disk Utility as this will be in operation to run the app, and Disk Utility cannot operate on a disk that has apps already running. To use Disk Utility:

Checking disks

Don't forget

Disk Utility is located within the **Applications** > **Utilities** folder.

Disk Utility

Don't forget

If there is a problem with a disk and macOS can fix it, the **Repair** button will be available. Click on this to enable Disk Utility to try to repair the problem.

Beware

If you erase data from a removable disk, such as a flashdrive, you will not be able to retrieve it.

1 Open Disk Utility then click the **First Aid** tab to check a disk

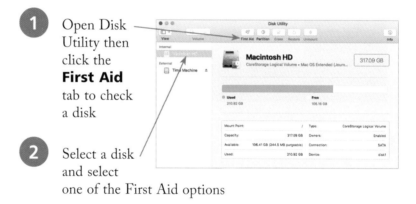

2 Select a disk and select one of the First Aid options

Erasing a disk

To erase all of the data on a disk or a volume:

1 Click on the **Erase** tab and select a disk or a volume

2 Click **Erase** to erase the data on the selected disk or volume

Erase

System Information

This can be used to view how the different hardware and software elements on your MacBook are performing. To do this:

1 Open the **Utilities** folder and double-click on the **System Information** icon

2 Click on the **Hardware** link and click on an item of hardware

System Information is located within the **Applications** > **Utilities** folder.

3 Details about the item of hardware, and its performance, are displayed

```
MATSHITA DVD-R  UJ-898:

Firmware Revision:  HE13
Interconnect:       ATAPI
Burn Support:       Yes (Apple Shipping Drive)
Cache:              1024 KB
Reads DVD:          Yes
CD-Write:           -R, -RW
DVD-Write:          -R, -R DL, -RW, +R, +R DL, +RW
Write Strategies:   CD-TAO, CD-SAO, DVD-DAO
Media:              To show the available burn speeds, insert a disc and
                    choose File > Refresh Information
```

4 Similarly, click on network or software items to view their details

```
Calendar                          8.0

Calendar:

Version:        8.0
Obtained from:  Apple
Last Modified:  16/09/2015, 16:17
Kind:           Intel
64-Bit (Intel): Yes
Signed by:      Software Signing, Apple Code Signing Certification
                Authority, Apple Root CA
Location:       /Applications/Calendar.app
```

Activity Monitor

Activity Monitor is a utility app that can be used to view information about how much processing power and memory is being used to run apps. This can be useful to know if certain apps are running slowly or crashing frequently. To use Activity Monitor:

Activity Monitor

1 Open the Activity Monitor and click on the **CPU** tab to see how much processor capacity is being used up

System:	1.03%	CPU LOAD	Threads:	719
User:	0.45%		Processes:	187
Idle:	98.51%			

2 Click on the **Memory** tab to see how much system memory (RAM) is being used up

MEMORY PRESSURE	Physical Memory:	8.00 GB	App Memory:	1.90 GB
	Memory Used:	2.94 GB	Wired Memory:	1.04 GB
	Cached Files:	1.30 GB	Compressed:	0 bytes
	Swap Used:	0 bytes		

3 Click on the **Disk** tab to see how much space has been taken up on the hard drive

Reads in:	86,144	IO ⌄	Data read:	2.65 GB
Writes out:	20,518		Data written:	530.0 MB
Reads in/sec:	0		Data read/sec:	0 bytes
Writes out/sec:	1		Data written/sec:	8.80 KB

Updating Software

Apple periodically releases updates for its software; both its apps and the macOS operating system. All of these are now available through the App Store. To update software:

1 Open **System Preferences** and click on the **App Store** icon

App Store

2 Click here to select options for how you are notified about updates and how they are downloaded

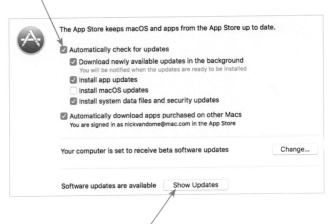

3 To check for updates manually, click on the **Show Updates** button

4 Available updates are shown in the Updates section in the App Store. Click on the **Update** buttons to update. If there are no updates available this will be stated, with the latest updates underneath

Software updates can also be accessed directly from the Apple menu, located on the top Menu bar. If updates are available, this is denoted by a red, circled number on the **App Store** link on the Apple menu, or on the App Store app's icon.

Check **On** the **Automatically download apps purchased on other Macs** box if you want to activate this function.

For some software updates, such as those for macOS itself, you may have to restart your computer for them to take effect.

Gatekeeper

Internet security is an important issue for every computer user; no-one wants their computer to be infected with a virus or malicious software. Historically, Macs have been less prone to attack from viruses than Windows-based machines, but this does not mean MacBook users can be complacent. With their increasing popularity there is now more temptation for virus writers to target them. macOS High Sierra recognizes this, and has taken steps to prevent attacks with the Gatekeeper function. To use this:

Hot tip

To make changes within the General section of the Security & Privacy System Preferences, click on the padlock icon and enter your admin password.

Click the lock to make changes.

182

1️⃣ Open **System Preferences** and click on the **Security & Privacy** button

Security & Privacy

2️⃣ Click on the **General** tab   General

3️⃣ Click on these buttons to determine which locations apps can be downloaded from. You can select from just the Mac App Store, or Mac App Store and identified developers, which gives you added security in terms of apps having been thoroughly checked

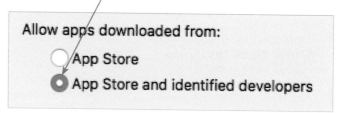

Allow apps downloaded from:
- App Store
- App Store and identified developers

Beware

If a password is not added for logging in to your account, or after sleep, other people could access your account and all of your files.

4️⃣ Under the **General** tab there are also options for using a password when you log in to your account; if a password is required after sleep or if the screen saver is activated; showing a message when the screen is locked; or disabling automatic login

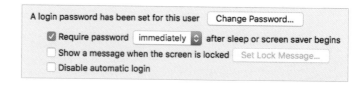

A login password has been set for this user   Change Password...
☑ Require password immediately ⬍ after sleep or screen saver begins
☐ Show a message when the screen is locked   Set Lock Message...
☐ Disable automatic login

Privacy

Also within the Security & Privacy System Preferences are options for activating a firewall, and privacy settings. To access these:

1 Click on the **Firewall** tab

2 Click on the **Turn On Firewall** button to activate this. Click on **Firewall Options...** to change settings for the firewall

3 Click on the **Privacy** tab

4 Click on the **Location Services** link and check **On** the **Enable Location Services** option if you want relevant apps to be able to access your location

5 Click on the **Contacts** link and check **On** any relevant apps that want to access your Contacts

6 Click on the **Share Mac Analytics** link, and check **On** the **Share iCloud Analytics** if you want to send information to Apple about the performance of your

MacBook and its apps. This will include any problems, and helps Apple improve its software and apps. This information is collected anonymously and does not identify anyone personally

A firewall is an application that aims to stop malicious software from accessing your computer.

macOS High Sierra apps are designed to do only what they are supposed to, so that they do not have to interact with other apps if they do not need to. This lessens the possibility of any viruses spreading across your MacBook. For instance, only apps that have the ability to use Contacts will ask for permission to do this.

Problems with Apps

The simple answer

macOS is something of a rarity in the world of computing software: it claims to be remarkably stable, and it is. However, this is not to say that things do not sometimes go wrong, although this is considerably less frequent than with older Mac operating systems. Sometimes this will be due to problems within particular apps, and on occasions the problems may lie with macOS itself. If this does happen, the first course of action is to restart macOS using the **Apple menu > Restart...** command. If this does not work, or you cannot access the Restart command if the MacBook has frozen, try turning off the power to the computer and then starting up again.

Force quitting

If a particular app is not responding, it can be closed down separately without the need to reboot the computer. To do this:

Beware

When there are updates to macOS these can, on rare occasions, cause issues with some apps. However, these are usually fixed with subsequent patches and upgrades to macOS.

 Select **Apple menu > Force Quit...** from the Menu bar

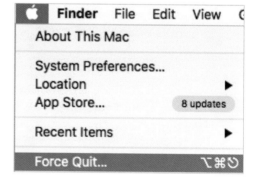

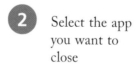 Select the app you want to close

 Click the **Force Quit** button

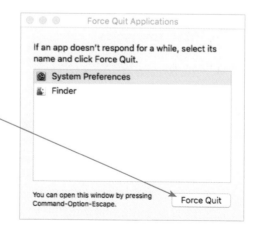

General Troubleshooting

It is true that things do occasionally go wrong with macOS, although probably with less regularity than with some other operating systems. If something does go wrong, there are a number of areas that you can check and also some steps you can take to ensure that you do not lose any important data if the worst-case scenario occurs, and your hard drive packs up completely:

- **Backup**. If everything does go wrong, it is essential that you have taken preventative action in the form of making sure that all of your data is backed up and saved. This can be done with either the Time Machine app or by backing up manually by copying data to a CD, DVD or flashdrive. Some content is also automatically backed up if you have iCloud activated.

- **Reboot**. One traditional reply by IT helpdesks is to reboot: i.e. turn off the computer and turn it back on again, and hope that the problem has resolved itself. In a lot of cases this simple operation does the trick, but it is not always a viable solution for major problems.

- **Check cables**. If the problem appears to be with a network connection or an externally-connected device, check that all cables are connected properly and have not become loose. If possible, make sure that all cables are tucked away so that they cannot be inadvertently pulled out.

- **Check network settings**. If your network or internet connections are not working, check the network settings in System Preferences. Sometimes when you make a change to one item this can have an adverse effect on one of these settings. (If possible, lock the settings once you have applied them, by clicking on the padlock icon in the Network Preferences window.)

- **Check for viruses**. If your computer is infected with a virus this could affect the efficient running of the machine. Luckily this is less of a problem for Macs, as virus writers tend to concentrate their efforts towards Windows-based machines. However, this is changing as Macs become more popular, and there are plenty of Mac viruses out there. So make sure your computer is protected by an app such as Norton AntiVirus, which is available from **www.norton.com**

Don't forget

In extreme cases, you will not be able to reboot your computer normally. If this happens, you will have to pull out the power cable and re-attach it. You will then be able to reboot, although the computer may want to check its hard drive to make sure that everything is in working order.

...cont'd

● **Check startup items**. If you have set certain items to start up automatically when your computer is turned on, this could cause certain conflicts within your machine. If this is the case, disable the items from launching during the booting up of the computer. This can be done within the Users & Groups section of System Preferences by clicking on the **Login Items** tab, selecting the relevant item and pressing the minus button.

● **Check permissions**. If you or other users are having problems opening items, this could be because of the permissions that are set. To check these, select the item in the Finder, click on the **File** button on the top Menu bar and select **Get Info**. In the **Sharing & Permissions** section of the Info window you will be able to set the relevant permissions to allow other users, or yourself, to read, write or have no access.

Click here to view Permissions settings

● **Eject external devices**. Sometimes external devices, such as flashdrives, can become temperamental and refuse to eject the disks within them, or even not show up on the Desktop or in the Finder at all. If this happens, you can try to eject the disk by pressing the trackpad when the MacBook chimes are heard during the booting-up process.

● **Turn off your screen saver**. Screen savers can sometimes cause conflicts within your computer, particularly if they have been downloaded from an unreliable source. If this happens, change the screen saver within the **Screen Saver** tab in the **Desktop & Screen Saver** preferences of the System Preferences, or disable it altogether.

Q

R

S